# Visi⊙nary Shamanism

"*Visionary Shamanism* is a beautifully written guide. There is a grounded spirituality to this writing, and the authors' ability to both express and celebrate humanity makes it accessible to everyone who is searching for a higher meaning."

MOLLY M. ROBERTS, M.D., PRESIDENT OF
THE AMERICAN HOLISTIC MEDICAL ASSOCIATION

"Star Wolf and Anne Dillon have birthed a highly stimulating book that will activate new dimensions of aliveness and inspire the successful living of our divine human potential."

LEONARD ORR, FOUNDER OF RE-BIRTHING BREATHWORK

"This highly readable book is a goldmine of fascinating material. It clearly demonstrates how past-life memories, including past-life knowledge, can spontaneously rise to the surface to be reexperienced and reenacted in places where we have lived before."

SABINE LUCAS, PH.D., JUNGIAN ANALYST
AND AUTHOR OF *PAST LIFE DREAMWORK*

"*Visionary Shamanism* reminds us to create from the future and not from the past. Through its many wonderful stories, ancient spiritual teachings are revealed, and clear guidance is offered as to how we can heal our past and clear the way to be the best self we are meant to be."

CHRISTINE R. PAGE, M.D., AUTHOR OF *2012 AND THE GALACTIC CENTER*

"*Visionary Shamanism* deconstructs current shifts happening on the planet. The authors provide us with the hopeful and fascinating fuel to ignite our hearts at an intuitive level and instigate the requisite inner shamanic journey each of us must make to solidify that change. It is the perfect read for the times we live in."

LAURA CARPINI, AUTHOR OF *BEAR SPEAKS: THE STORY
OF 7 SACRED LESSONS LEARNED FROM A MONTANA GRIZZLY*

# Visionary Shamanism

## Activating the Imaginal Cells of the Human Energy Field

Linda Star Wolf
and
Anne Dillon

Bear & Company
Rochester, Vermont • Toronto, Canada

Bear & Company
One Park Street
Rochester, Vermont 05767
www.BearandCompanyBooks.com

Bear & Company is a division of Inner Traditions International

**Library of Congress Cataloging-in-Publication Data**

Wolf, Linda Star.
  Visionary shamanism : activating the imaginal cells of the human energy field / Linda
Star Wolf and Anne Dillon.
      p. cm.
  Includes bibliographical references and index.
  Summary: "Shamanic practices to access your spiritual blueprint, communicate with the
universal mind, and transform into your highest spiritual self"—Provided by publisher.
  ISBN 978-1-59143-131-2 (pbk.) — ISBN 978-1-59143-939-4 (e-book)
  1. Shamanism. 2. Aura. 3. Spiritual life. 4. Wolf, Linda Star. I. Dillon, Anne, 1958– II.
Title.
  BF1621.W655 2011
  299'.93—dc23

                                                              2011032922

Printed and bound in the United States by Lake Book Manufacturing
The text stock is SFI certified. The Sustainable Forestry Initiative® program promotes
sustainable forest management.

10   9   8   7   6   5   4   3   2   1

Text design by Priscilla H. Baker
Text layout by Virginia Scott Bowman
This book was typeset in Garmond Premier Pro with Mason Alternate and Gill Sand used
as display typefaces

To send correspondence to the authors of this book, mail a first-class letter to the
authors c/o Inner Traditions • Bear & Company, One Park Street, Rochester, VT
05767, and we will forward the communication, or contact Linda Star Wolf at **http://
shamanicbreathwork.org**.

*We dedicate this book with infinite gratitude to the One Source*

*and its healing power, which comes to each of us through*

*the always available and ever abundant imaginal cells*

*that regularly renew the hearts, minds, and spirit of all humanity*

*throughout time and beyond.*

*We also dedicate this book to a beautiful Visionary Shaman,*

*Wolf Clan Grandmother Twylah Nitsch, Yehwehnode—*

*She Whose Voice Rides The Four Winds.*

# Contents

cᐯɔ

# FOREWORD

*Visionary Shamanism* is a clear and simple book about a very complex and thought-provoking idea—we must download information from the future to be totally present and fully embodied now. The authors comment, "On our planet we've lost the natural ability to travel shamanically into the other worlds, to go into altered states, and to find the *messenger from the future* that can show us what we need to know now for our present-day circumstances" (my italics). I agree! That is, because we are currently experiencing the peak of our long evolutionary journey, we must seek future knowledge in order to obtain a sense of direction.

In this wonderful idea, *Visionary Shamanism* bridges two parts of my own work—research into past-life regression under hypnosis and my Mayan calendar research in *The Mayan Code*. Given this, I'd like to share my thoughts about this very timely book.

Star Wolf and I share a deep background. We have both explored our past selves very comprehensively; we are both now exploring our future selves passionately; and we were both initiated into the Seneca Wolf Clan by Grandmother Twylah Nitsch, who was an amazing elder, visionary shamanic leader, and teacher of the Wolf Clan teachings. She was a medicine grandmother for both Star Wolf and me and is now on the other side, working with both of us. In fact, Star Wolf and I sense that Gram put us together so that I could write the foreword for this book.

As you will read in these pages, for many years Star Wolf accessed her past selves to gain inner wisdom. Additionally, she birthed a breathing technique, Shamanic Breathwork, that she uses to help people let go of the past and come more fully into the present moment. In my case, I experienced one hundred sessions under hypnosis in order to explore my past lives, which I documented in *The Mind Chronicles*. By doing this research, I awakened a deep knowledge of these past selves, which is the basis of my work as a teacher and ceremonial leader.

At this point, many other people have already accessed past selves and learned from them. They often found that problems in their current lives could be traced to their past lives. When those past lives were delved into and their traumatic events explored and worked through, blocked energy was liberated. These releases healed emotional blocks, relieved pain, and eradicated inappropriate judgments. Such efforts allow people to be much freer in the Now.

As valuable as this may be, the more important idea that Star Wolf offers here is that it is time to draw knowledge from our *future* selves. It is this concept that I will now discuss because I know it is quite a stretch for most people.

I stumbled on the idea of seeking wisdom from future selves by accident when I discovered the research of the Swedish biologist Carl Johan Calleman. He discovered that the *tun-based* (360-day) Mayan calendar suggests more closely spaced events as time advances, culminating in a dynamic cluster of incidents in 2011. During this one year, the evolutionary wisdom of 16.4 billion years unfolds in a simultaneous release of nine levels of organic growth, which we humans can use as a new frequency band that is beyond time.

How fitting it is that *Visionary Shamanism* would appear right now! It is loaded with much essential advice on how to accomplish the birthing of our long-awaited future selves that were seeded so long ago—our *imaginal cells,* our spiritual blueprint. *Visionary Shamanism* teaches us how to access and work with the messenger from the future, an inner intelligence that knows how we can make the quantum evolutionary leap. How can we put this idea into some kind of context?

In the Seth books, Jane Roberts attempts to help readers experience simultaneous time. Her characters have adventures during which they interact in the past, present, and future; they explore these time states simultaneously. In my opinion, Roberts was only partially successful because the world wasn't yet ready to hear what she had to say. However, now we are ready for this idea, which will open doorways into many dimensions, into the *multiverse,* for those who can navigate into the future.

The authors show how communing with future selves provides direct access to information that can tell us what we have to do to choose the future life we want. When we do this, the authors say, we are accessing our *imaginal cells,* "our unfolding self that is eager and ready to be born into the world." This beautiful and rich idea can help us to let go of pain and addiction from the past so that we can create the new Earth.

*Visionary Shamanism* is filled with wonderful ideas about *how* to locate and access these mysterious imaginal cells, and readers may find that these cells activate just by reading this book. They did for me, which has already given me new and valuable sources of wisdom.

I'd like to complete my thoughts by linking this book to my own understanding of the Mayan calendar's meaning and ending based on Calleman's research. As already noted, Calleman's interpretation of the Mayan calendar reaches back 16.4 billion years, to the birth of the universe. He proposes the progressive acceleration of time and predicts the fruition of our species during 2011. You may wonder why our analysis of this ancient calendar really matters. It does because, like all movements that result in radical change, only a very few people lead the transformation during the final phase. Soon thereafter, the movement becomes functional in the everyday world when many millions learn to live in new ways.

As part of my research into Calleman's theory, I studied other sacred cultures to see if they had the same idea about evolution going far back in time and accelerating exponentially as the years advance. To my utter amazement, I did find that many of them, such as the Vedic of India, seemed to realize that humans would be participating in an evolutionary spiral that is culminating right now.

*Visionary Shamanism*'s insights about time and evolution are much simpler than the complex calendar theory, which is why I believe this book is very important for us. The authors believe that past shamans contacted the messenger from the future for guidance, which is what I think the ancient cultures that discovered spiral evolution were also able to do. The Maya even called their calendar diviners "visionary shamans," and they created fantastic art that shows them having their visions.

In other words, the messenger from the future is the same being as the *genus loci* embedded in the calendar! Through my access to ancient wisdom, I have come to understand that this messenger may be our last access to guidance now, because *time is going away.*

The end of time is difficult to imagine, yet the heralded end of the Mayan calendar is not about the end of our species or our planet; it is about the end of time! When you find the essential now—the nexus point of past, present, and future—you have located this fabled messenger from the future.

Use this book to tune in to the imaginal cells within yourself, because they are the deepest wisdom in the core of your soul, which vibrates eternally in the very center of your heart.

BARBARA HAND CLOW

Barbara Hand Clow is an internationally acclaimed ceremonial teacher, author, and Mayan calendar researcher. Her numerous books include *Awakening the Planetary Mind, The Pleiadian Agenda, Alchemy of Nine Dimensions, Liquid Light of Sex,* and *The Mayan Code.* She has taught at sacred sites throughout the world.

## My Journey with Linda Star Wolf in the Making of This Book

*I came to know Linda Star Wolf when I edited her book* Shamanic Breathwork *in my position as an editor at Inner Traditions • Bear & Company. I have always been interested in esoteric teachings and healing work and soon was participating in Shamanic Breathwork workshops led by Star Wolf and her husband, Brad Collins. In the process, she and I became good friends and had many interesting discussions about the nature of breathwork, why it is so effective, and how sorely it is needed in our world today to awaken our inner visionary shaman. From those discussions, this book, which conveys the voice of Star Wolf, was happily born.*

ANNE DILLON

*Nut, ancient Egyptian goddess, transmitting star energies*
*and sacred purpose to Geb, her partner on Earth*
*(Illustration © 2011 by Kris Waldherr, www.KrisWaldherr.com)*

# A Message from Nut, the Great Egyptian Sky Mother Goddess

*N*ut, the sky mother goddess of ancient Egypt, woke me up one morning before sunrise while Jupiter was still very bright in the dark night sky.* I felt Nut's shimmering presence downloading powerful information into my energy field. She arched her beautiful, indigo blue, star-filled body over me as I lay in my bed, caught in between the worlds, only half awake. Nut conveyed her message of sacred purpose to me through electromagnetic waves that filled my mind and heart with many strong images and emotions.

Over the past year I've repeatedly heard the same inner message: "It is time not only to heal the past but also to learn from the future." I've spent the last twenty-nine years focused on healing the past and moving toward a "bigger picture." I've done an enormous amount of inner work, both personally and professionally. I've concentrated on ridding myself of dysfunctional, addictive patterns, and I have assisted others in

---

*The visions articulated in this book came to me as direct revelatory experiences and, as such, may not conform exactly to traditional knowledge of ancient Egypt and its rich and mysterious culture.

finding freedom from their inner demons. I hold the belief that in some way we all have addictions that keep us from being who we really are and who we came to Earth to "be."

The Shamanic Breathwork process I developed and that emerged from my own healing journey has proved to be an amazingly beneficial tool in helping people who are ready to heal the past as well as download visions of their potential future selves. Through the healing power of the breath, people are able to drop very quickly into an altered state and, essentially, time-travel back to all the situations through which they've experienced soul loss and taken on negative energies that need to be released. These negative energies have often kept them stuck in their present-day lives as if the past was still their living reality.

Until we let go of our attachment to our pain body (our ego's need to hold onto pain as a way of feeling alive), we will continue to spin around and around in the same old pattern, and not much progress will be made. Daily dedication and a willingness to heal our past will automatically move us forward on the spiral path of transformation. When we let go of old, outworn patterns that no longer serve us, we can energetically free up space in our psyches so that learning from the future becomes not only possible but the most probable outcome.

Many people write, teach, and talk about releasing their past programming. One of the main messages of this book is that the time has indeed arrived for humanity to give equal attention to our *future* programming. This future programming is held within our archetypal DNA as well as our physical DNA and can be even more compelling than our past programming, once we surrender our ego's agenda and open to our soul's true purpose. This is not an easy task.

The Shamanic Breathwork process accelerates the transformation of consciousness by raising one's awareness of the time line of past, present, and future realities. It reaches deep within the psyche to resolve hidden conflicts and unfinished business from the past, whether rooted in this lifetime or another. Simultaneously, the breathwork journey moves us beyond the limits of the "little self," which likes to play reruns of our past as if it is still our present. When we wake up and realize that our egos are unconsciously addicted to pain and suffering, the opportunity opens for our future self to download into the present so it can manifest now.

Make no mistake about it, the future self is very real, and many alternative realities are available for our imaginations to grab hold of. The imaginal selves, which together form the perfectly realized archetype of who we are really meant to be, exist in conjunction with the past selves but they do not always manifest in our current existence. When we begin to actively feel their pull within us, they are moving into our present life. In other words, our imaginal selves are eager and ready to be born into the world. They need our conscious cooperation to come into being, and as a result of their emergence, we will grow in self-awareness and wisdom. Without the assistance of our imaginal selves, our development will consist of a long succession of woeful experiences.

Suffering is very real on our planet. Genuine pain is all around us: in war-torn countries like Iraq and Afghanistan; in countries where environmental disasters have left millions of people without food or shelter; in situations where disasters resulting from human error have trashed the environment.

For those of us fortunate enough *not* to experience these external disasters directly, much of what we suffer tends to be self-imposed as a result of our ego attachments to past patterns of dysfunction, which mainly are unconscious. Many years ago I was taught that we have two choices: we can focus on the problem or become a part of the solution. While I do not advocate staying in denial or practicing spiritual by-pass by ignoring the problem and denying our human emotions, I also know the pointlessness of reliving the past over and over in a self-defeating manner.

The world around us is a reflection of our inner state of being. As we collectively move into the new eon, we need to open to a much bigger vision for our future. This is an evolutionary shift that has been predicted by religious, spiritual, and shamanic traditions for thousands of years. The common motif or prophecy has it that a time would come when we would need to wake up and see that we are all connected and a part of the world's greatest challenges and opportunities for transformation. As we collectively shape-shift our consciousness away from addiction and into planetary service, we will begin to live and give from the fullness of our sacred purpose, simultaneously healing the world around us as we heal ourselves.

The earth and all its beings are calling out to the heart of humanity to heal itself and open to a larger reality. This is not a time for staying half asleep but for fully awakening and taking creative action in our lives. Staying stuck in the past is about addiction; opening to the future is about embodying the full measure of our energies of love and sacred purpose.

My personal spiritual commitment is to continue to rid myself of the immaturity and selfishness that blocks my soul's true purpose. *I don't believe in accidents; however, I do believe in divine appointments.* My hope, my prayer, and my faith is that we will all awaken from our deep slumber before it is too late. It is time not only to imagine a new Earth, but to create it. We must each find the love in our hearts that will inspire and motivate us to fulfill our unique role in helping to reshape reality. We begin by taking responsibility for changing ourselves and helping to open the portals in order to birth a higher love and wisdom, or, as the great master Jesus said, create Earth as it is in Heaven. It is time for humanity to shape-shift into its future self now!

LINDA STAR WOLF

# Acknowledgments

*W*e would like to thank all the staff at Inner Traditions • Bear & Company, especially Jon Graham, Jeanie Levitan, and Jamaica Burns Griffin. As well we would like to thank Helena Nelson-Reed for creating the beautiful cover to our book and Kris Waldherr for the use of her wonderful illustrations.

Star Wolf would also like to thank all the visionary shamans who have directed her to awaken the shaman within:

Mammy Jones, my grandmother, who taught me to honor the living spirit within all things and to pay attention to my dreams

Margaret Jean Moore, my cousin, who introduced me as a teenager to the magic of the tarot and divination

Edgar Cayce, "the sleeping prophet," who was born thirty minutes from where I was born and grew up; I never met him in person but his legacy has touched my life since early childhood

Florence, who helped shepherd my early sobriety

Jacquelyn Small, my beloved mentor and breathwork teacher who helped me to transform my life and to remember who I am

Mel Sudh of AIWP who ordained me as a minister and challenged me to step up to the plate to become a visionary leader

Barbara Hand Clow, Wolf Clan Sister, thank you for your powerful visionary work and beautiful foreword for this book

Laura Wolf, the world's most amazing personal assistant and spirit daughter

Ruby Falconer, my wise advisor and soul sister

The people of the amazing Isis Cove Community and the magical Blue Mountains that I call home

The members of the Sedona Intensive Training Group who served as my faithful Shamanic Cheerleaders throughout a year of sharing the budding ideas birthed within this book

Anne Dillon, my friend and coauthor, who believed in this book even before I did; my heart is full of love, admiration, respect, and gratitude for you

Brad Collins, my beloved visionary husband, partner, and best friend, who not only believes in my visions but assists me in their manifestation on Earth

Grandmother Twylah Nitsch, my spiritual grandmother, who helped me find myself again by guiding me to live my truth and reconnect to the sacred Earth and Blue Star energies of higher love and wisdom

Normandi Ellis, whose depth of insight and understanding about ancient Egypt helped to inform my visions of that land

Nicki Scully, an extremely gifted alchemical and shamanic teacher and healer, who, as a major catalyst in re-uniting me with my inner oracle, was and always will be my true shamanic sister

And, finally, to the thousands of kindred spirits, who, for more than three decades, have allowed me the great honor to witness and participate in the shamanic journeys that have transformed you into visionary shamans that you are

# 1

# STAR WOLF'S JOURNEY

*Walking between the Worlds*

*O*ne of my most profound experiences of walking between the worlds occurred just before my twelfth birthday—and it changed my life forever. I was an only child who was very attached to my maternal grandparents, and I frequently stayed for days at a time at their place while my young parents worked many long hours to make a living. My grandparents—Mammy and Pappy, as I referred to them—lived right down a rural road from us in western Kentucky. I was extremely close to my grandmother; to me, she was like a second mother and more. As I look back at our relationship, I realize we had a "soul contract" and were meant to be together for my important formative years, which acted as the template for the rest of my life.

I don't know how it began, but as far back as I can remember, my Mammy always taught me to talk about my dreams in the morning; we would discuss them and consider what they might mean. This seemed so natural and normal that I thought that every child did the same thing.

Mammy was of Dutch Irish descent, and she taught me about the natural world of trees, plants, rocks, and animals, much like a Native American grandmother would do. She was very much into fairies, leprechauns, and mythical creatures. She taught me to respect nature and to believe that everything was full of spiritual essence—that I could talk with the stones, the trees, and the animals, indeed, with all things found in nature.

We talked about dreams coming true and being able to see into the future with dreams. While she didn't call me psychic, she did say that I had "special gifts." She thought I had an ability to read what she called "signs"—premonitions, omens, those kinds of things. She confided in me that my mother had these gifts as well but had mainly repressed them due to an unfortunate incident when she was a little girl in which in a dream she had seen her beloved dog go mad (get rabies) and someone cut off its head. (When a dog is suspected of having rabies, its head is cut off and sent away to be tested.)

Apparently shortly after she told her mother (my Mammy) about this dream, it came true. From that day forth Mammy said that my mother denied and shut down her abilities. Mammy encouraged me not to do that, no matter what. My abilities were a gift from God, she explained, and they were to be used wisely to help others and sometimes even myself. She said in time I would learn how to use this gift and others that I had and not to worry about it.

I was taught from a very early age that when I went into the other worlds in the dreamtime, I could walk in that world and gather impressions from an energy field that today's science might call "a creative matrix." When I woke up I could then bring some of the energy back with me to create things. In other words, I could learn from the future, although I didn't call it that back then. If I really wanted to bring the dream's information back into *this* world, I would simply focus on my dream as I was starting to wake up, and I would make it very clear in my mind's eye before I opened my physical eyes. Then I would write it down, draw a picture of what had happened in it, or talk to someone about my dream the next day, before I ate breakfast, before I had a chance to really "ground" myself back in this dimension with the body's process of eating and digesting a meal.

If I didn't want to bring back my impressions, I simply refrained from focusing on or discussing my dreams until after I had eaten. This allowed the dream's energies to dissolve back into the other realms of existence. In other words, giving special attention to and speaking out loud about the dream experience helped to create a pathway between the worlds, which made it easier for the dreams to manifest in my everyday reality. This reminds me of the scripture verse in the Bible that speaks about "the word made flesh."

One night a few months before my twelfth birthday, I had a dream that Mammy died. In my dream I saw my grandmother's clock. It was a wind-up alarm clock with bright green numbers on it. The dials glowed in the dark, and I was able to see the time of her death and the details of her passing, which took place in a hospital. This didn't seem plausible because Mammy hardly ever went to a doctor. In her words, she didn't trust them. She was much more likely to use some sort of home remedy to heal whatever was ailing her—or me, for that matter. However, it was so disturbing to see my precious Mammy die in my dream that when I woke up in the morning I felt very troubled.

Mammy was already well into cooking me breakfast when I came into the kitchen. The air was filled with the delicious smell of her home-made biscuits and milk gravy with fresh henhouse eggs frying alongside of my Pappy's smokehouse bacon. When she saw me, she immediately sensed my unease and knew something wasn't right. She asked me what was wrong while putting my plate of food in front of me. Instead of diving in to my breakfast and being my normal chatty self, eager to share one of my many dreams from the previous night, I responded that I really didn't want to talk about anything, especially about my dream.

This puzzled Mammy because she knew that wasn't like me at all, so she kept questioning me, and finally she persuaded me that no matter how horrible my dream had been, if I told her about it, then everything would be all right. I trusted Mammy so much and I was so distressed that I ended up telling it to her. She never flinched and kept asking me questions until she felt that I had gotten it all out of my system and that I was feeling better. She ended the conversation by telling me that everything would be all right and to eat my breakfast—which I was able to do after getting "all the worry out of me," as she put it.

Mammy had reassured me by saying she would always be with me no matter what and not to fret, and so, with a child's innocence, I let it all go. It was only a short time later that Mammy suddenly became very sick. At Thanksgiving she started going downhill, unexplainably so, and true to form, she refused to go to the doctor. She said that the best thing for her illness was bed rest, although it was very atypical of her to rest in bed for any amount of time. She was always active and busy, either in the kitchen, in the garden, or with the farm animals and such. I was staying with her quite a bit at this point because it was the holidays and my folks were working a lot. First it was Thanksgiving, then her birthday, then mine, and then Christmas.

My Mammy had taught me to watch for "the signs" of things to come. Some of the other members of my family didn't believe in signs and said they were old-time superstitions, but Mammy was a firm believer in messengers from the other worlds. She believed that certain signs meant that death was near or that big changes were afoot.

For instance, a picture of a deceased family member, a loved one, falling off the wall for no particular reason was a sign. It might be seen as an indication that the spirits were close by and were coming near to support the approaching death and transition to the other side of their loved one, or to guide them through a difficult time ahead. During this period my senses heightened and I started to see some of these signs. For example, a picture of Mammy's deceased parents fell off the wall and the glass cracked. If the glass cracks, that's another indication that a portal has opened and the time is near for a big change, such as death. Sometimes if birds fly into your windows and are killed or if they actually enter your home, it is a sign that some sort of death is approaching.

More than one bird flew into the window of Mammy's living room when she was becoming increasingly ill. One also suddenly flew into the house when we opened the door, and we had a lot of trouble getting it out. I remember the worried look on her face that day, but again she took great pains to reassure me that everything would be okay.

As Mammy's health steadily declined, many of these omens continued to occur. She turned fifty-five a few days before my twelfth birthday, on December 14. She finally went to the hospital because it had become increasingly clear that something was very wrong. The ambulance took her away, and she never returned home.

After running tests in the hospital, it was discovered that she had a ruptured appendix and her body was poisoned as a result. My parents tried to protect me from knowing how ill she really was. Coupled with this, at that time young children were not encouraged to be visitors at the intensive care units of our county hospital, so I was unable to spend any real time with her. After she checked in to the hospital, I got to see her only once more for about ten minutes, and I was shocked to see how swelled and awful she looked.

Mammy was hooked up to all kinds of tubes and machines and could barely speak, but she managed to say how pretty I looked in the new blue mohair sweater that she had given me money to buy for my birthday. Part of me just couldn't accept that she was dying, and I think my parents were in denial too. As the grand matriarch of our family, Mammy had always seemed invincible. I told her I loved her and walked out the door, not realizing it was the last time I would ever see her alive in this life.

A few days later, on New Year's Eve at the age of fifty-five, she died in the hospital, in the very way that I had envisioned her passing in my dreamtime experience. It wasn't until many years later, when I was in my late twenties, that I would remember this event in its entirety in a therapeutic session and realize its full impact on my life. At that time I consciously came to grips with the turn my life had taken at her death. It had been a turn toward deep despair and addiction, because I had blamed myself, as a child, for her untimely death. I had become convinced that, had I not told her my dreamtime experience, she would have lived.

The experience of losing my beloved grandmother, who was also my best friend, soul companion, and a teacher who knew how to effectively guide me with my "special gifts," was a devastating loss at a time when I was entering puberty, a significant turning point of my life. I carried the wounding of her untimely death for a very long time, and this led me down some very dark roads. I became lost and angry, and I acted out my pain and suffering in unconscious ways during my teen years in the 1960s, losing the innocence of my childhood rather rapidly following her death. Most of my talents went underground as I suppressed them with drugs and alcohol and other addictions. Some people use substances to "get high"; however, I felt like I mainly used substances to escape my pain and to feel normal. It would be several years before I would find my way back from the underworld and follow the path of remembering who I really was.

# 2

# BECOMING THE
# VISIONARY SHAMAN

*I* believe that we are all born with a powerful shamanic spirit. Like the rest of the natural world that we are so deeply related to, we are given many wonderful shamanic gifts from our divine source. One of the most powerful gifts of all given to us from the creator is the inner knowing and wisdom that informs us when it is time to let go, to die, and to be reborn into a whole new level of consciousness.

Certain people, like me, appear to be born with an extra dose of natural shamanic talents, such as the ability to travel between worlds the way I frequently do. This is a large part of my sacred purpose, and I believe it's why I chose my particular grandmother: she knew how to nurture and provide just exactly what I needed for my spirit to flourish and grow within my body and for my special gifts to emerge. I accepted many years ago that I am on Earth in part to assist and guide others in connecting to their shaman within, particularly now as we are moving into the Aquarian age and everyone can open to their inner shaman. We can open to our inner shaman by utilizing tools like Shamanic Breathwork, which helps us learn how to develop the nonlocal mind in order to avail ourselves of ancient wisdom as well as to receive the fertile downloads coming in from the future realms of consciousness.

Developing the nonlocal mind allows us to access different places and different times with our thoughts, instead of being limited to the here and now. The nonlocal mind is not restricted to past, present, or future events but can travel between all three realms. It is the field that prayer, miracles, visions, and revelations draw from, including the sense of déjà vu. The laws of synchronicity are active in this kind of shape-shifting reality, and cause and effect are not what they seem to be in linear time.

According to many of the great spiritual traditions—Hinduism, Buddhism, esoteric Christianity, and some indigenous teachings—everything already exists and, in a manner of speaking, has already happened on some imaginal plane of existence; *everything already is*. I refer to this as Isis, or is is. It's not *going* to happen; it's not that it *will happen* someday. However, because of our innate need to focus on times and events sequentially in order to have a "human experience," we are created and designed to see the past, present, and future in a linear space-time continuum. They are reference points that we have collectively created so that we can exist in a spatial reality where our life lessons are learned and synchronistic occurrences congregate to give us clues about the truth of our powerful shamanic natures.

Some of us know how to gaze into the future to read the Akashic Records, which are variously described as a cosmic library or a kind of supercomputer whose esoteric data include everything that has ever happened in the cosmos and everything that ever will. Psychotherapist and author Michael Newton has written extensively about his experiences with clients who, in a state of deep hypnosis, have been able to access these records in order to make decisions about their own life's path.*

A person in a deep hypnotic state may be able to access a state between incarnations in which they travel to the Akashic Records to select a future life—all human lives that ever were and ever will be are recorded there. In so doing, the soul also chooses which sex to be,

---

*Michael Newton's books include *Journey of Souls: Case Studies of Life Between Lives* and *Destiny of Souls: New Case Studies of Life Between Lives.*

selects a family to be born into, and familiarizes him- or herself with the lessons that a particular life will impart. In this way, the nonlocal mind can look into the past, the present, and the future.

I know that I frequently see things that help me make decisions about the future. People call it precognition or intuition. If I'm driving down a road and become a little lost, then come to a fork and wonder which way to go, I will often receive a strong intuitive sense about which turn to take. Later on I might hear that there was a major accident on the road I chose not to take. Or I might meet someone or come across something that affects my life in a meaningful way, and I have a sense about it at that time. That's really not only seeing into the future, but trusting the future, because there's no way to rationally know, at that present moment, what is what. In the past, magicians, wizards, priestesses, oracles, and high priests were often advisors whose gifts of prophecy helped rulers make decisions about how to most effectively lead their people into their collective future.

One of my main reoccurring visions over the years has directed me to embrace my inner shaman and to become an opener of the way, so that others can consciously travel between the worlds and learn not only from the past but also from the future. Visionaries like Buckminster Fuller, Henry Ford, and Albert Einstein could easily draw upon this ability. Barbara Marx Hubbard, a well-known teacher of spiritual evolution, refers to this energy as the imaginal cells. She has greatly popularized the notion even though Deepak Chopra has been given credit for coining the phrase, drawing upon scientific findings and research to do so.

The imaginal cells are the very valuable part of us that already have an existence in another realm. In some ways it is as if they have already lived in the future; they are the seeds of the future that are downloading into our human energy fields and into our human levels of consciousness.

In some ways you could say that the imaginal cells represent our human potential, but it's actually more substantive than that because our imaginal cells already exist within the matrix. You might think of it as software that is now being downloaded into form. This is a very powerful concept because it shows us how miracles happen; it shows us how we can bring everything together into one dimension and one realm.

One of the quickest ways that I know of to open up our psyches and actively engage with the imaginal cells, allowing them to enter, is to learn how to shape-shift from our ego agenda to our soul's purpose—to the bigger oversoul. We must learn to employ what I refer to as shamanic psychospiritual methods (a phrase I coined to describe the work we do), such as Shamanic Breathwork, on a more regular basis, which will assist us in traveling beyond the limits of the "little self" to encounter simultaneous realities. In his book *A New Earth: Awakening to Your Life's Purpose,* Eckhart Tolle speaks about a place beyond our "pain body." He describes journeying to a place where we see ourselves through the eyes of our soul or through our spiritual self, rather than through the ego mind.

If we can tune in to the imaginal cells, we can open ourselves up more easily and allow the imaginal cells to come in and create. That's what they do over time anyway, and they do it with or without our consent. However, when we *consciously* invoke them and actively surrender to the process of change, we accelerate the process of allowing the imaginal cells entry so that we can bring our newest incarnations in more quickly and speed up our evolutionary process as it pertains to consciousness and making the quantum leap.

Many forward-thinking people on the planet right now believe that we must take this step to ward off the extinction of the human race and the extinction of life as we know it. Time is speeding up, and the planet and its inhabitants are crying out for the changes that must be made, not only to survive but to make the evolutionary leap that is ours to make in the grand scheme of the universe.

To embody shamanic consciousness in everyday life is to fully appreciate and learn from everything around us: the elders, the children, the animals, and all of nature. We look to the heavens and the Great Star Nations, and we also look deeply into our own soul's wisdom to access all we have learned from our journey through time and space and beyond.

Walking in shamanic awareness in the Aquarian age is not necessarily about knowing the "correct" order for calling in the four directions or the "exact" number of stones to be placed in the medicine wheel, or the "right" way to behave in a particular ritual or ceremony. Awakening the shaman within is much more about learning how to heal oneself by knowing oneself. We all contain shades of light and dark, and what we come to learn as we do our shamanic work is that we do not judge these nuanced aspects of ourselves. They are neither good nor bad, they just are: the light, the dark, no difference. The visionary shaman is not only interested in advancing the evolution of powerful spiritual traditions by respectfully honoring what has been, but also in standing on those teachings as foundations while continuing to dream the dream forward in an upward spiral of spiritual wisdom. It is time to ask ourselves what the twenty-first century visionary shaman looks like and to take a long hard look in the mirror while we are listening for the answer to our question.

Instead of seeing ourselves as either accidental creations or as children of God, I now have the clear vision that we are divine and need to see ourselves in this different light. When we learn to accept our multidimensionality and multiuniversality, we become responsible for our creations in the world of time and space. In so doing, we actually become co-creators with God, living out our destiny as universal humans and actively co-creating the future with the Great Mystery. At this point, no matter where we find ourselves in this vast universe, at least we will know that we are and always have been home.

# 3

# GRANDMOTHER
# TWYLAH NITSCH

## *The Download Star Wolf Received on the Day of Grandmother Twylah's Passing*

*M*y burgeoning interest in the shamanic world eventually led me into a deep exploration of Native American traditions and other earth wisdom teachings when I was in my mid thirties. This brought me to a gifted elder by the name of Grandmother Twylah Nitsch, Wolf Clan Grandmother of the Seneca Tribe, who first appeared to me while I was in a guided inner breathwork journey that altered my state of consciousness. During this inner journey, Grandmother's spiritual presence made itself known. When she stroked my head and called me Gentle Star Wolf, it had a life-changing effect on me.

It took me several years to actually track down Grandmother Twylah in the outer world. When I finally arrived at her home on the Cattaraugus Indian Reservation outside of Buffalo, New York, she asked me (rather firmly) what had taken me so long (she had appeared to me several years prior to my actual visit). I was quite shaken and answered that perhaps I would have found her sooner had she given me directions to where she lived!

Grandmother Twylah Nitsch was born in 1913 on the Cattaraugus Indian Reservation. Raised by her grandparents, medicine man Moses Shongo and his wife, Alice, they trained her to become a lineage holder of the Seneca wisdom and a leader of the Wolf Clan Teaching Lodge. This role was prophesied before her birth and was passed on to her after her grandfather's passing when she was just nine years old.

Daughter of a Seneca mother and an Oneida-Scots father, Grandmother Twylah was a direct descendant of Chief Red Jacket, a renowned Seneca orator whose discourses are still studied by scholars today. The Seneca are among the founding members of the Iroquois Confederacy, originally a five-tribe group known as the Five Nations, which later became the Six Nations. The Seneca are the acknowledged philosophers of this assemblage, now called the Iroquois League, or the League of Peace and Power.

Grandmother Twylah's clan, the Wolf Clan, teaches the wisdom, philosophy, and prophecy of Earth history, namely that all creatures— all creation—are members of the one family born of Mother Earth, and that our destiny is to reclaim that oneness. Gram, as she was fondly called by many, brought students into her home to learn the ancient ways firsthand. She formed the Seneca Indian Historical Society, a school without walls, and began holding councils and numerous workshops and disseminating her teachings through a home-study correspondence course. In April of 1999 she received the prestigious Living Treasures of North America Heritage Award in recognition of her life's work.

## WOLF CLAN ENERGY

I spent several years learning the ways of the Wolf Clan energy. This included the cycles of truth emanating from my vibral core (the personal power center or essential core self that can never be broken and connects us each to our source) and walking in trust, stability, dignity, love, and gratitude. Gram gave me lessons on finding, naming, and talking to the stone people (rocks). She spoke to me about the wisdom of the animals (creature teachers) and the standing people (trees). She also spoke to me about the Great Star Nations—the many different Native American people who believed that they originated from the stars. She told me, with a twinkle in her eye, that we were all from the stars and that we came here to learn how to be "real human beings." She said that if we could just see the invisible ones who were waiting in line to get an "Earth suit," we would thank our lucky stars for our bodies and our journey around the sacred wheel of life!

The Pathways of Peace and the Cycles of Truth were two of her foundational teachings, and they focused on entering the silence of our "within," finding our true power by living from the truth of our vibral core, and radiating the soul qualities of wisdom, integrity, stability, and dignity—which, in turn, would create inner peace and happiness in our lives. Gram passed on what her beloved grandfather had taught her: that following the twelve Cycles of Truth and the Pathways of Peace would help us to preserve our wholeness, walk in balance, and fulfill our life's mission. We must learn, honor, know, see, hear, speak, love, serve, live, work, share, and be thankful for the truth.

Following the Pathways of Peace means living in harmony with this ancient philosophy. Gram believed in peace and frequently spoke of becoming a peacemaker—first in our own hearts, then in our families, and then in the world around us. She believed it was the responsibility of all of us to carry the seeds of peace and the message of peace into every aspect of our lives and the world. One of her favorite sayings was "All for one and one for all."

The path of the wolf encouraged me to step more fully into my role as a visionary pathfinder and way-shower for others. Grandmother Twylah asked me to pass on what I was learning from her, in addition to my own inner experiences. Gram always encouraged me to be true to my vibral core—my inner divinity—and to listen to my heart and spirit. Perhaps this was her greatest teaching to me. She used the words "Go to your within, within, within. This is the place of your vibral core, the essence of your true being."

I once said to her, "Gram I honor and love you and all that you have taught me, but my path is to take what has meaning in my life and integrate it with the other paths and lineages that speak to me; I will not teach it exactly as you do." She responded, "There is only one Grandmother Twylah, and I don't want to be cloned!" She told me she knew my heart and trusted who I was, and knew that my work would reach many people on the planet. She said that was why she had called me and so many others to her, in order that the sacred teachings might live in the hearts of many. She knew that I would not lose the heart of what she was sharing with me.

She went on to explain that to travel the path of the wolf is to be a type of scout, a pathfinder, a way-shower. She said the wolf spirit person was a thinker as well as a healer, and could navigate her way on the shamanic path through multiple levels of consciousness. She said the wolf person would have a vision and follow it with her whole heart, and then take that lesson and knowledge back to the rest of the clan. Wolf energy is also about being able to see the bigger picture and envision a better world; the wolf can be both a visionary and a prophet. The wolf is a natural teacher and shares what it has learned with others, thereby passing on the wisdom to future generations.

## CONNECTING THROUGH LOVE

Gram passed into the other realm on August 21, 2007, and I must share with you some of the magic that occurred on the morning of her passing, at the precise time that she passed away. My husband, Brad, and I were at the Still Meadow Conference and Retreat Center on the Clackamas River in Portland, Oregon, an old Emissaries of Divine Light community. This is a very holy and sacred place. The emissaries did a lot of sacred work here. The sanctuary was built following the principles of sacred geometry, and the land was attended to in a very special way. In addition, a magnificent creek runs through the property. Also on the land are two giant Douglas firs, which are each over nine hundred years old; these are very rare. They're the two guardians of that property, and they're magnificent.

Brad and I went to Still Meadow to lead a workshop on the alchemy of change and the spiral path. One of the women who lived there had been part of the old Emissaries community, and on the night that Brad and I arrived, she told us about the center and the old trees that graced the property. She said that we should make a trek into the woods at some point to see them; our whole group should.

We agreed, but at that point it was raining, we had been traveling all day, and I was due to lead a workshop the entire next day. So it was much to my surprise when, the next morning at about 4 a.m. I awoke with a start and began to vibrate as if electricity was running through my entire body. I had the distinct feeling that someone or something was calling me to go outside and walk down the path into the forest to visit the two Douglas fir trees (one is a Grandmother and the other a Grandfather) in the sacred wood. (More than seventy acres of natural land, creek, and forest have been preserved at Still Meadow.) As my friends well know, I am not typically a morning person, so to even *contemplate* going outside, given the prevailing conditions, was difficult for me.

And while this was something that I might have done at the age of forty, I was then fifty-five, and as previously stated, I had a whole day's workshop ahead of me. But when I got the call, outside I went, in the dark, in the woods, in the rain, to find the two trees by myself.

I did find the two elder trees, and I sat between them, and I prayed with them. As I did, they showed me a vision of the spiral path of time running backward. They showed me the history of life on this planet, and they showed me everything that had evolved. They showed me that everything that had been born had died and been born and died and been born again in an evolutionary sort of way. When I saw this, I felt the grief of everything that had passed away, but at the same time, I also felt that things had evolved as they were meant to.

The spirit of the trees told me that the grief I was feeling was a natural and normal thing, that it was right and dignified to mourn the passing of something that had been in form and was now formless, something that had gone back to the Great Mother, back to the great cosmic void. However, they also showed me that in the last few hundred years, time has been speeding up. They showed me that species were being destroyed and were going extinct—not because of evolution but because of the destructiveness of humankind.

And they showed me a vision of all of the trees around them that would have been as big as they were had they survived. Incredulous, I asked them, "How did *you* survive?" And all they would say to me was "Through love." There must have been someone who stepped in and said, "Leave these two trees"—someone who loved them enough, all that time ago.

"Through love."

They showed me everything that had passed unnaturally over the past one hundred, one hundred and fifty, two hundred, six, seven, eight hundred years, and it was tremendously sad. I found myself weeping and weeping and weeping. And then they showed me, in my own life, the things and people who had passed away naturally and unnaturally from my own life. I then flashed on Grandmother Twylah and my maternal grandmother, Callie, who I called Mammy, two of the most important and influential people in my life, whose loving presence I felt guiding me in that very moment.

I stood and walked a few feet to place my hand on the Grandfather tree. I found myself saying aloud, "Please, Great Ones, help me to stand tall and strong with dignity, speaking my truth, living with integrity, sharing what I have learned and my gifts with the world in a good way. Help me to weather the storms of life as you have, and to grow upright reaching to the stars and putting down strong roots to nourish my life and soul as well as the lives of those around me. Help me to keep my heart open, alive, and awake, and to renew it over and over again, never becoming stagnant or dulled by my own complacency. Help me not to be overwhelmed with the negativity of what may be occurring in the world around me."

As I said these words, I felt an amazing vibration of renewed energy pouring through my heart center and knew I was being initiated and healed by these great beings in the woods and by the spirits that were present. I plucked two hairs from my head and offered one to each of the great trees, and then I proceeded on my walk. I was guided out of the woods, across the field, and past a huge stand of bushes filled with blackberries. I've never seen so many ripe, luscious berries, and I couldn't resist having breakfast right there in the field. I continued my walk, now moving deep into woods that looked very much like a primeval forest. I would not have been surprised to see a brontosaurus munching on ferns and the moss that hung from the tall tree limbs! I slowly made my way down the side of a beautiful creek bank on old, worn, slippery steps. As I did so, I was reminded of the creek behind the pasture and woods at Grandma Twylah's house on the Cattaraugus Indian Reservation outside of Buffalo, New York.

Many years ago Gram sent me to the river to spend the day searching for healing stones. She gave me very specific instructions on how to find them and told me to bring them back for her inspection. She taught me to notice how many sides the stones had, told me what their numerology was, and instructed me on how to listen to the message hidden deep inside their ancient bodies. She then told me to sit outside all night by a small fire circle that was partially hidden and encircled by dense trees. I sat with the stones, my elder teachers, under the moon and a night sky filled with more stars than I had ever seen. And I listened to the stones as they gave me their wisdom teachings.

I now found myself gathering healing stones in the manner that Gram had taught me so many years before. I felt like a happy child gathering the stones and listening to those who called to me as I joyfully hopped barefoot in the creek.

Suddenly I had a sensation that I often have when something wants to download into my conscious awareness from another realm. I closed my eyes and stood still in the middle of the creek—for how long I don't know. It was then I saw a large wheel of light and a blue star. The blue star pulsed, and I heard a voice that instructed me to build a new type of wheel for healing and transformation. I asked if it was to be a medicine wheel and was told yes, but it was not to be called a medicine wheel, because it was coming from the future and the Great Star Nations.

It was to be called the Blue Star Shamanic Wheel of Transformation (or Blue Star Wheel, for short). I was told it was representative of the Aquarian visionary shaman energy that has been birthing onto the planet through Venus Rising* and other organizations and individuals who were opening to learn from the future as well as passing on the wisdom of the ages. It would serve as a guiding path to deeper healing and transformation and provide a map for the cycles of change for many people who would come to walk, meditate, pray, or do ceremony within the wheel. Once familiar with the wheel, individuals would then be able to hold it in their awareness and return to it through their imagination, receiving the healing transformation and energy downloads as if they were actually in its physical presence.

I became very excited as I returned to my outer awareness and couldn't wait to get back to my husband, Brad, and share all that had happened on my unexpected early-morning vision quest. I told him about my morning, and he too became very excited. We realized that we wanted to bring this message to our group members, who, synchronistically, happened to be at the retreat for our once-a-year training there. We asked for and were given permission to build the first Blue Star Wheel at Still Meadow (it has since been moved to a private property in Portland).

I then returned to my room to prepare for the morning's Shamanic Breathwork journey. I uncharacteristically decided to quickly call my home phone to see if there were any messages—something I usually do at

---

*The Venus Rising Association for Transformation is a 501c3 nonprofit organization that was founded in 1996 by Linda Star Wolf. Star Wolf developed the Shamanic Breathwork process as a synthesis of the shamanic stream of work throughout the ages, in conjunction with modern integrated psychological principles. Currently she and her husband, Brad Collins, codirect Venus Rising; it is located at the Isis Cove Retreat Center in the mountains of western North Carolina. For more information, see "About Venus Rising Programs" at the end of this book.

the end of the day while traveling. On my voice mail was an urgent message to call Grandma Twylah's son and daughter-in-law, Bob and Lee. My heart raced as I shakily called them and learned of Gram's passing.

While I spoke with Lee, it slowly dawned on me that it was Gram Twylah who had awakened me in the wee hours before dawn and called me to the elder trees and the elder stones in the creek. She always spoke so lovingly and respectfully of the trees, the stones, the creek beds, and the animals. I realized the grief I had been feeling was deeply connected to her passing and the inner knowing that all things and beings must eventually pass from this reality into the Great Mystery. It was her voice that had come to me, along with the voices of the great trees, to reassure me and guide me back to my renewed vision and to my heart, and to my commitment to the path that I had chosen—or perhaps I should say that had chosen me—so long ago.

It was her words that reminded me to live in trust, to stand tall, and to have the courage to speak the words of truth and living wisdom learned from the cycles of change and from the sacred experiences of life. It was her voice that reminded me that there is a well-worn spiral path from this reality to all other dimensions, and from Mother Earth to the Great Star Nations. And it was her voice that spoke to me as I stood in the sacred waters of Richardson Creek among the ancient stone Grandmothers and Grandfathers. It was she who instructed me to create a wheel that would incorporate the best of the old ways with the new teachings that are emerging as we enter the age of the Aquarian visionary shaman.

Lee told me that a ceremony was going to be held for Gram at her location and also among Gram's friends all over the world. It was due to happen at the same time that our group at the retreat center would be undergoing a Shamanic Breathwork journey. I told Lee we would call in the energies and that we would connect our ceremony for Grandma Twylah with theirs.

A bit later, in the group, I tearfully shared the news of Grandma Twylah's passing and my bittersweet shamanic experiences of the morning.

Everyone was profoundly touched and went into their breathwork journeys carrying with them the magic of all that had happened that day.

Music is always part of our shamanic journeying, and that day was no exception. But much to my chagrin we could not, no matter how many times we tried, get our prerecorded music to play on cue. In fact, we couldn't get *any* CD to play on the CD player—except for one: "Sacred Spirit," the only Native American music CD that we had brought with us. Every time Brad hit "Disc 1" on the CD player, it would flip to "Disc 4" and start to play "Sacred Spirit." We even took it out of the CD player and tried other CDs in the Disc 4 slot, but as fate would have it, nothing else would play!

Finally I leveled a look at Brad and told him, "Nothing is going to work, except 'Sacred Spirit.' Gram is here. A few minutes ago we invited her spirit to join us in our breathwork, and this is the music *she wants us to play for her*!" Sure enough, as soon as Brad put "Sacred Spirit" back into the Disc 4 slot, it played just fine, and so that was the CD we used for the entire session.

Almost everyone in the group had Grandma Twylah visit them during their breathwork journey; she gave each person a message of some sort. Some were quite humorous, I might add, and all were deeply meaningful.

Magic also happened back in North Carolina where Venus Rising's headquarters is located at the Isis Cove Community and Retreat Center.* I had quickly called my son, Casey, to let him know of Gram's passing and asked him to let the folks in our community know about the 2 p.m. EDT ceremony. Following is an the e-mail I received later that day from Ruby Falconer, one of our Isis Cove Community members and Venus Rising's business manager and colleague.

---

*Isis Cove Community and Retreat Center was founded by Linda Star Wolf and Brad Collins in April 2003. They live and work at Isis Cove, offering transformational retreats, shamanic initiations, and Shamanic Breathwork training programs. The community consists of several individually owned homes; the members of the community are mainly teachers, healers, and guides of various kinds.

Hi—

I did get your message regarding Grandma Twylah's passing. Kathy, Windraven, Karen, and I gathered on the deck at 2 p.m. to hold a sacred space* for her. Just as we were gathering, it started to thunder. We smudged, and then stood together, holding hands, and each of us gave thanks to her for the work she did while on this earth and for the gifts she gave to us. None of us had met her in person, but we all feel indebted to her for the teachings she's given us through you, through the Medicine Cards and the Sacred Path Cards and in so many ways. We thanked her sincerely from our hearts. We thanked her for the Wolf Clan, and I told her that we are the Aquarian Wolf Clan—that we are the ones who will carry her teachings into the new age and that we will not let her teachings die.

We thanked her for Isis Cove and told her that we believe that Isis Cove exists because of her and the teachings that she gave you. We thanked her for everything she's given to us through you. Kathy pointed out that we had chosen, without thinking about it, to gather on the deck, where the Wise Wolf Women had gathered.

After that we gave Gram a really big wolf howl.

And Star Wolf, it poured rain, and the skies cracked open in huge peals of thunder as though the Thunder Beings were welcoming her soul and acknowledging our prayers. It truly was amazing.

We felt your presence and the presence of everyone in Portland, and we felt the presence of other Wolf Clan members—many of whom we do not know in person—scattered all across this country and the world.

And it poured rain.

Love, Ruby

---

*Holding space is the directing of thoughts, energy, and attention to a person, place, thing, or event to commemorate it or help shepherd it in some way. For instance, breathwork is normally practiced in pairs, with one person doing the breathing and the other holding space for the breather.

Later on that day Casey called and told me about the miracle of the rain, which had not been predicted in western North Carolina. Our area had been experiencing a drought for many weeks. He was convinced that Gram Twylah had something to do with it. Casey said, "Mom, right at the time all the ceremonies were happening on both sides of the country for Gram, I went out to look up at the sun and send Grandma Twylah and you some energy. These huge clouds gathered. It thundered, the sky broke open, and it poured rain like crazy. Then the clouds dispersed and the sun came back out almost as suddenly as it had disappeared, and it has been sunny ever since." He echoed Ruby's words when he told me "It really was amazing."

Gram continues to wake me up to tell me more about the Blue Star Wheel and how she wants it built as well as the Blue Star teachings. As always, she has very specific instructions as to how it is to be done. I have always felt a strong heart connection with Gram, but now it is as if we have gone from dial-up to wireless! I feel the deep sadness of her passing from this physical plane while at the same time I feel a deepening of her love and wisdom in my heart—and I know this will continue to grow. Grandma Twylah and her vision, her spirit, her teachings, and her magic are alive and well in the hearts of all those who love her. Those of us she called her "wolfies"—her family members, students, friends, and Wolf Clan Soul Family members who were fortunate enough to have heard her coyote laughter and see the twinkle of her eyes—can say we truly have been blessed.

For now I must go and teach, and yet I know Grandma is close by, whispering in my ear, "Don't forget to trust" . . . "Remember trust has an 'us' in it" . . . "We weren't meant to do it alone" . . . "All for one—one for all!"

God bless you, Gram.

# 4
# Activating ·Our· Imaginal Cells

*At the still point of the turning world. Neither flesh nor*
    *fleshless;*
*Neither from nor towards; at the still point, there the*
    *dance is,*
*But neither arrest nor movement. And do not call it*
    *fixity,*
*Where past and future are gathered. Neither movement*
    *from nor towards,*
*Neither ascent nor decline. Except for the point, the still*
    *point,*
*There would be no dance, and there is only the dance.*

FROM T. S. ELIOT, *FOUR QUARTETS,*
"BURNT NORTON," PART II

*P*art of us *always* knows where we are on our journey, the part that keeps track of all our experiences without judgment. Our inner record-keeper archives the transcripts of all our lessons learned. I refer to it as our essential core self. As mentioned in the last chapter,

Grandmother Twylah Nitsch talked about this and taught me, and a multitude of others who sought her out, about our essential vibral core.

Sometimes we look around and, depending on what's going on in our life, we say, "What was I thinking when I decided to come to this planet?" But when we remember, we realize that our inner knowing brought us here so that we could embrace our destiny as Star Children. On some level we understood that we were we were coming here to learn about the nature of love, the deep, rich connection to a powerful life-force energy that is shamanic in nature, which understands the power of the light and the dark, which understands the power of the spiritual realms, the invisible realms, and which understands the deep richness of the human experience.

## THE SHAMANIC PATH OF TRANSFORMATION

What does it mean to become an Aquarian visionary shaman, to live from the shamanic psychospiritual perspective, and to embrace the spiral cycles of change? The shamanic psychospiritual path is a path of direct experience to our own lives, the mystical and the mundane. It is not a religious path; however, it can be brought into any spiritual or religious tradition that you may already be involved with. This path of the heart and mind has become my chosen spiritual path, one that leads me to the direct source of my being. I have chosen to follow this path of direct experience because it encompasses, for me, the esoteric heart of all traditions and then some. It is the merging of the ancient wisdom teachings inherent in all traditions—everything that has already been— with the new, cutting-edge, consciousness paradigm and information downloads from the future, the quantum leap of being that is calling to us from our imaginal cells.

We can use the caterpillar as a model for our discussion of imaginal cells. Science tells us that the caterpillar, like us, has a regular cellular structure as well as a cellular overlay composed of isolated imaginal cells. Gradually, as the caterpillar naturally grows and evolves, the imaginal cells become greater in number and threaten to override the old structure. The caterpillar interprets this as an attack on its immune system. It tries to rid itself of these imaginal cells, and it is able to do so as long as the imaginal cells remain isolated units. But when they band together, as they do as part of the growth spurt process, they become too strong for the immune system to break down; their collective power is too great. As they gather momentum by forming cell clusters and exchanging information, they become the dominant growth paradigm of the organism, until pretty soon there is no stopping them, and they gloriously morph into the new creature that is the beautiful butterfly.

That's the scientific delineation of the process. But what does it *feel* like for the organism—whether a caterpillar or a human being—that is undergoing the transformation?

Human beings are much like the little caterpillar that's walking around, munching on leaves, and happy in its sphere of being—interacting in a harmonious way with the natural world. Then one day something happens. The caterpillar experiences a restlessness, you might say, a dissatisfaction with just eating leaves and being on the ground. It wants to do something entirely different, but it doesn't yet know what exactly that is. I can imagine it suddenly feels a yearning, a holy longing, for some bigger purpose than what its life has been thus far. It's time for it take an action, perhaps one it has no understanding of cognitively but feels instinctively.

Let's look at this miracle of metamorphosis. The word metamorphosis means to undergo a great change. One of the best examples of metamorphosis is illustrated by the life cycle of the Monarch butterfly. The Monarch lays her almost microscopic eggs on a plant, where they mature into tiny caterpillars in about three days. This is known as the larva stage, wherein the baby caterpillar consumes more than its own weight every day and takes three weeks to grow to full size. It then attaches itself to a solid surface, such as the limb of a tree, and in an amazingly short amount of time (approximately two minutes), it turns itself into what is known as a chrysalis. Thus begins the pupa stage of its transformation. It secretes a liquid from its body and covers itself with this liquid in order to create an alchemical container for its own dissolution.

The caterpillar then releases chemicals stored within its body and begins to turn into a mushy substance. Out of this mushy goo all the internal organs, body, head, and beautiful wings are formed. In about a week the transformation is complete, and the Monarch butterfly is born! It has created its own safe and special place, a tomb or a womb—they're different sides of the same coin—so that it can die and be reborn.

And just as the caterpillar created a protected space for renewal, we too at our Venus Rising Association for Transformation and Venus Rising University for Shamanic Psychospiritual Studies have fashioned safe and sacred places. Our Isis Cove Retreat Center is a place where we and others can undergo deep transformation. It's really important to understand how to spin or walk the spiral path, how to become ungrounded, uprooted, and to take ourselves apart; the caterpillar inherently knows how to do this. A secretion of its body is designed to dissolve its form, and as it dissolves itself, its little eyeballs fall off, its tail falls off, and it turns into mush. Simultaneously, emerging out of that muck is a new creature that's growing little humps on its shoulders and acquiring colors and new eyes and a new way of being and developing.

All these things are happening in ways we don't consciously understand at all. And it's probably really uncomfortable and painful at times. If we could ask the caterpillar and she could answer, she might say, "You just don't know what I am going through! I didn't know what was going on! My eyeballs just fell out and I melted away into mush! Oh no!"

But death to the caterpillar is birth to the butterfly.

However, at the time the caterpillar is undergoing the process, it doesn't know that—it doesn't know what's coming. It's not like it dies and then it becomes the butterfly either—it's all happening simultaneously. The old form is dying while the new form is being born. Life and death are complementary opposites that travel together. And this whole planet and everything on it is shamanic at its core. The shamanic world is about life, death, and rebirth, and the alchemical process everything and everyone goes through on our planetary evolutionary path of transformation, growth, and expansion.

Rebirth is the divine third, the third thing that springs from the union of the two. Rebirth is beyond the original form of life and death; it is the next level of consciousness that we can't even imagine when we are feeling like the little caterpillar just crawling around. Where did the urge and urgency come from that motivated the caterpillar to stop eating long enough to climb high up onto the branch, where, once anchored and wound up in its vessel for transformation, it began the process of dissolving itself?

Did it have any idea at the beginning of its journey that someday it would fly, and in order to do so it would have to undergo a shamanic journey of death and rebirth?

Do we?

Imaginal cells represent what has already happened in "heaven," if you will; they exist as thought forms in the archetypal blueprint of the invisible world. They live in the "Field of Plenty" that Grandmother Twylah often taught about—the place where all of creation arises from the cosmic soup. Just as the caterpillar is capable of and designed to morph into its true self, the butterfly, so too can we morph into our most highly realized state of being, by activating our own imaginal cells.

Several spiritual evolutionists today are speaking about the imaginal cells that exist in our vibral core. They believe that even though we are not consciously aware of these imaginal cells, they are present nevertheless. Does this concept challenge the notion of free will? I'm not going to say that free will doesn't exist because I don't believe that *everything* is predestined in life. However, I believe that there is a divine plan, and a divine blueprint, an intent, for our spiritual and human evolution. It's really an important part of who we are. Why would all of the natural world appear to have an original blueprint and intention for its destiny and future form and that not be true for human beings as well?

Imagine that one day the little caterpillar—when it has finally reached its new form, even though it's still kind of mucky—begins to struggle for life, feeling that it has to be born. It gradually breaks open the chrysalis, and when it comes out it sits there for a while and rests, drying off its wings for a moment, and then . . . something happens. An incredible urge, it doesn't even know what it is, and it doesn't even have the word "fly" in its vocabulary, but imagine this incredible urge that propels it to take a leap and to fly like crazy, and suddenly . . . *it has a much bigger world!* Instead of just a little area where it can crawl only a few inches or feet or yards, it can fly hundreds, even thousands of miles, very high, very low, over mountains, over streams, tasting the nectar and pollinating the flowers in all this beauty, offering its gifts back to the world in a much bigger and more profound way than it ever imagined.

I wonder if we are not just reveling in the beauty of the story, but in the reminder that this is a journey that we, as humans, are also making, from the caterpillar and the unconscious into something that is much, much bigger. This shamanic journey, of being born and then evolving to the next level of consciousness, is ongoing. We do not just weave that web or create that chrysalis once.

However, if we're resistant and afraid of change, we are going to shut down, contract, close up, and hold on to all the forms that we have, whatever they might be. We're not going to let these old forms dissolve, because we're afraid that if we do, the next one either won't be waiting for us or if it is, we won't like it or it will be dangerous or it won't feel comfortable, or we won't feel safe. There are a lot of things that we're potentially afraid of.

Every one of us can think of something that we're afraid to change. We're afraid to sell our house, leave a dysfunctional relationship, quit our job; we're afraid to let go of certain securities that we have; we're afraid to cut our hair or grow our hair; we're afraid to express our opinion—what will people think? With anything that requires a change in our lives, we have to go through a very similar process to the one demonstrated by the caterpillar. Nature abounds with many shamanic examples from our elder brothers and sisters.

Why were we feeling the need to change anyway? What could propel us into undertaking such major upheavals in our lives?

Well, my personal and professional experiences have shown me that for many of us, it becomes too hard to remain the same, that some sort of suffering is affecting our lives. Why doesn't it feel comfortable anymore? Our ways of being feel comfortable for *a while*. I believe that the imaginal cells call to us to change, and whether we register it, whether we can put words to it, whether we make it conscious or not, they call to us nonetheless. Some part of us knows to answer that call, just like the trillions of cells in our bodies that are right now in the process of dying off and renewing themselves.

How do they know that it's time to die? We can say they're programmed, but what does that mean? It means they have little signals. "It's time to die." "Okay." "Time to be reborn." "All right." That's happening, over and over again, from the physiological aspects of ourselves to our emotions. Have you ever been down in the dumps, and you indulge in that feeling for a while, and then all of a sudden somebody calls you and you snap out of it? How do we know when we've had enough? We know because something inside us calls us and says, "Enough already."

The point is to understand that we have natural, organic mechanisms in our emotional world, in our physical world, in our intellectual and spiritual worlds that tell us when to change. As one of my teachers once said, "If God only wanted us to have one emotion, that's all we'd have been given." Our emotional intelligence helps to signal us when it is time for a change. Everything that exists in the world is sacred, if only we have the eyes to see that, but we often mistake the natural shamanic process of death and rebirth as being indicative that something is wrong or that something has been done in error.

# THE SACRED JOURNEY OF LIFE:
# THE LIGHT, THE DARK, NO DIFFERENCE

In the shamanic work that we do, both the light and the dark are sacred. This means that we find blessings in birth, in death, and in all the stages in between. Life is a journey; it is a process. So the anger, the sadness, the grief, the disappointment, the frustration, the confusion, the joy, the excitement, the passion, the creativity—all are part of being a fully embodied human being.

In my other books I have identified what I refer to as the alchemical map of five shamanic cycles of change. Each cycle is ruled by a dominant element—be it water, earth, fire, air, or spirit—and as we work on ourselves, one cycle gives over to the next. The natural world is always changing, as are we, and for this reason, nature is an integral part of Shamanic Breathwork. Each of these shamanic cycles of change also correlates with a shamanic initiation, which came to be called the Shamanic Healing Initiatory Process, or SHIP, facilitated by Venus Rising's staff. Each of these five initiations (the Five Cycles of Shamanic Consciousness and the Spiral Path of Alchemical Transformation, the Family of Origin, Dancing with the Shadow, Embracing the Divine Beloved, and Discovering Sacred Soul Purpose) builds upon the one preceding it and leads journeyers to a higher level of shamanic consciousness and wholeness in everyday life. Teachings, readings, exercises, and a Shamanic Breathwork session are embedded within each initiation. They are designed to create fertile ground and sacred space for monumental, transformational shifts in people's lives. We have repeatedly witnessed the miraculous during these intensive process groups.

Grandmother Twylah frequently liked to speak about becoming a "real human being" instead of just a "human doing." Years ago, my dear breathwork teacher Jacquelyn Small encouraged me to continue on my path of being an authentic self and being more soulful. She taught me an invaluable lesson: part of being authentic is being able to own our psychological processes, as funky as they might be sometimes, and our family of origin patterns, which are not just from this lifetime, by the way. Even if you don't believe in reincarnation and don't feel that you have family of origin patterns from other lifetimes, we have a whole DNA lineage that we are still evolving from—that we *do* know. We don't even have to know our parents in order to be a lot like them or repeat their patterns—both negative and positive.

Here is an example that reminds us of just how connected to patterns in our ancestry we can be: Monarch butterflies can migrate up to three thousand miles to spend the winter in Mexico. Even though these butterflies never meet their parents, they are able to fly to the same tree in Mexico their parents or grandparents wintered at the year before. There have even been documented cases in which it has taken three generations of butterflies to complete the round trip.

Just like the butterfly, we too have an ancestry. We have our very specific family of origin—the siblings and the schoolteachers and the parents and the significant others who we grew up with. The deep programming attendant to these experiences of growth has taken place in our physical and psychological worlds, beginning in the womb at conception and continuing through the gestation experience through to the actual birth of our little human bodies and spirits onto this planet. And the entire process is important: what was happening to our mother while she was pregnant with us; what was happening with our father, whether he was in our life—even his absence can still be felt. What happened on the day of our birth and what happened immediately following our birth? Everything that happens to us throughout all of this touches our lives and penetrates our energy field by permeating all of our chakras. And not only do our chakras and our energy fields take on the various aspects of our human experiences, so do the cells of our bodies.

With trauma, there is a shock to the light body and to the auric energy field. I often refer to this as a Shamanic Kodak Moment. The cells of our physical bodies experience this shock and receive an imprint. This imprint, which is trapped energy, can be very difficult to permanently erase. The energy of the trauma goes into thousands of cells in our physical bodies as holographic photographs and the shock waves of these energy snapshots travel in vibrational frequencies throughout our emotional bodies. In fact, our emotional bodies take in the energies of the experience, which triggers our brain chemistry and creates the encapsulation of those experiences in the very flesh and tissue and bone of our bodies. In addition, how we're thinking about it, how we're interpreting it, and how we're trying to make meaning of what's happening is encapsulated as well.

You can imagine a fetus or a baby or a child or even a young adult trying to make meaning of something that feels horrible or abusive or ecstatic or wonderful. It is a complex process to assign meaning to the information we receive from our outer surroundings. This takes place not only in the brain, even though we've been taught that thinking happens only in the brain. We now know, through research, that every part of our body thinks. Every part of our body feels and thinks and reacts.

All of these parts of us are responding to our experiences in the outer world. We have physical, emotional, and mental bodies. We also have etheric and auric bodies. We are penetrated by these energies that are coming in all the time from both our outer and inner experiences. We are multidimensional beings going through cycles of change on a multitude of levels, and we have the incredible shamanic ability to travel among all these bodies or worlds of information and assign meaning and purpose to everything.

As multidimensional beings we are walkers between the worlds and have the ability to be aware of existing in many worlds at once. We are able to transform consciousness, to move to higher and lower levels, to integrate all the worlds together, and to access the future and the past and the present. This constitutes the ability to be a time traveler and a shape-shifter, moving from caterpillar to butterfly, from life to death to rebirth, traveling to higher levels of consciousness, and being in touch with nature.

## THE NETERU, THE FOUR MESSENGERS

The word *nature* comes from the word *neter,* meaning "god" or "goddess," or "the divine world," as the Greeks saw it. The word *nurture* comes form the word *nature.*

At one time spirits of nature were honored and worshipped by many different traditions on a widespread basis. They weren't thought of as merely wind or water or fire or earth. They were thought of as gigantic forces that came from the One Source of the universe, the universal mind and heart. They were considered to be powerful forces in the universe and were associated with many of the gods and goddess of ancient Egypt as well as Greek and Roman deities.

As the word changed from *neter* or *neteru* to *nature,* we, in our continuing evolution, grew away from some of its deep power, and we lost the understanding of how this deep energy connects to our own power. In growing up, we humans evolved culturally away from nature, and now we treat it with disrespect.

It's analogous to how we might look at our parents when we're teenagers. They say, "If you knew what I sacrificed for you!" In the same way I can imagine that the elements of water, earth, air, and fire might say, "If you only knew the millions and billions of years that we worked together so that you could have life and evolve on this planet to where you are today."

The great trees stand and breathe so that we can breathe. Water, which makes up 75 to 80 percent of our body, purifies and cleanses us, and it never says, "Do you know what I'm doing for you?" Not one plant or animal that sacrifices itself so that we can eat begrudges us the offering.

Native American hunters, before taking the life of a bear or the deer, would say, "Forgive me, brother or sister," and then they would take the life, because doing so was essential to their survival. But they had respect for nature and the life they were taking. This is reflected the hunting scenes of the film *Avatar* in which Neytiri teaches Jake Sully how to hunt in a sacred manner and then comments on his "clean kill."

Indigenous people who lived close to the earth and in harmony with the natural cycles of life believed that whatever they ate, they would become, and whatever manner in which they took the life, whether that of a turnip or a deer, whatever manner in which they harvested a vegetable, or gathered berries from a tree, or ate grapes from the vine—the energy of the action was taken in along with the nourishment. If the animal died a violent, disrespectful death, they would ingest the spirit of that violation.

If we really were conscious and aware of our relationship with our natural environment the way the Native Americans were at one time, there is no way that we would continue to process "food" in the inhumane way that we do, whether genetically modified or raised in a cage.

Even though a lot of us are against the manner in which food is manufactured today and don't want to be a part of it, too many of us are still eating in an unconscious way; we're just not able to adjust our habits and put into practice what we've learned. However, awareness is changing, thanks to media attention and documentaries such as *Food, Inc.*, which really takes the gloves off. We need to continue to evolve consciousness around so much of what we have previously been taught was all right. We need to find the determination and the commitment so that we can create real change in the world. This is about waking up and taking responsibility for the changes that we really need to make at this time on our planet.

By getting back in touch with nature, with real nature, our human nature, we can nurture ourselves and the world around us. It's kind of like when kids grow up—they are finally able to appreciate their parents. This is where a lot of us are with nature now. We acknowledge nature and say, "Okay, I know we thought we didn't need you, but we do." Even though, in an occasional rare moment, we may have appreciated a beautiful sunset, the rhythmic calm of the ocean, or the whisper of wind in the highland pines, we are now experiencing more than just brief interludes. We are finding our way back and realizing that we are one with nature after all. The elements that nature is composed of are the elements that we're composed of!

We're coming back, if you will, to the neteru, to the gods. And as we come back into this place of honoring our human nature, we begin to understand that human nature is not evil. When someone does something unethical, the behavior might be dismissed as "just human nature." The implication is that human nature is evil, but I don't think that's true. Raw forces exist within us that may erupt—survival instincts, let's say, or territorial instincts—but I don't believe those self-serving forces define us. I think our truest human nature is to be in touch with nature, with nurture, with the neteru, and with the gods, and to have a true appreciation for who and where we came from.

## THE GREAT MYSTERY OF THE UNIWORLD

The neteru are part of who we are; however, they are not *all* of who we are. A larger force exists, a bigger universal life force; some call it the grand universal mind. Grandma Twylah Nitsch called it the Uniworld, or the One World, or the Great Mystery. I would say to her, "Would you please tell me what the Great Mystery is? Can you explain it to me? I want to know all about it." She would smile and reply, "Now, Star Wolf, if I told you what the Great Mystery is, it wouldn't be the Great Mystery, would it? Ha!"

Then she would laugh and say, "It's the unnamable and the inexplicable, and yet it's something we know very well deep down inside of us, because it's where we came from; it's alive in us. It's in our very cells. All that we have and all that we are came from that Uniworld, that One World."

She taught me that the Uniworld, the One World, is the great matrix of life. It exists as a precursor that forms the great matrix of invisible imaginal cells. She called it the Field of Plenty, where everything lives and emerges before being in form on planet Earth. When this Field of Plenty articulates itself into a form of matter, it descends and takes on a thicker vibration and a slower vibration in order to manifest. Everything comes from that place, and then divides, at least on this planet, into the categories of earth, air, water, and fire—in some combination.

The word *matter* derives from *its* original word, *mother*. *Mary* is another word for *matter* and *mother*. *Mary* is derived from the Egyptian word for "beloved" (usually a wife but not always a mother). *Mother* and *matter* are derived from the Egyptian word for the vulture mother Mut. This association is very sacred, if you think about it, but this concept of matter, or mother, in some religions, particularly the more fundamentalist ones, became demeaned over time. To be of the mother or to be in matter or to be in form became an abomination; it became a sin.

The life of the flesh is a potential minefield of sin, according to some fundamentalist religions, which advocate a lifestyle that follows the straight and narrow: don't make waves, keep your eyes on the prize, have a goal, plan ahead, have 2.1 kids and two cars in the garage, which is behind the house, which is behind your white picket fence. Don't expect too much, and continue to conform to this pattern and don't have a lot of change or chaos in your life and then if you're really lucky and you've done really well, one day you'll die and go to heaven or nirvana or paradise or whatever you want to call it, and there you will get your reward, maybe, if God decides you've earned it during the course of your upright life.

It's a pretty sad way to live, but that model has been put out for us to follow. Something may have gone wrong in your life: your perfect marriage just didn't work out—you had a great partner and a lovely wedding and a fantastic honeymoon and got three toasters but at the end of the day, it just didn't work out—or your dream job blew up in your face, or your baby was born with autism. The point is that things don't always turn out the way we want them to. Reality contradicts our intentions, and often what we get is the opposite of what we want, and wish, and hope for.

Often when this happens we undergo a period when we try to decide if this is just a lesson and we need to work through it by staying in it (the shaky marriage, the challenging job), or we need to move on.

A man in one of our therapeutic groups offered up his personal story. He talked about how, in his early thirties, he was a CEO at a very successful and wealthy company in San Francisco. In 1989, when the earthquake hit, he woke up. He saw the devastation around him and realized that life was short and fragile.

As a result, he quit his job and went traveling for a while. The corporation that he worked for begged him not to go. They offered him a really sweet deal, which included a professional relocation to Hawaii. Do you know what he told them? "Thanks but no thanks." He was conscious enough to realize that the earthquake had been a wake-up call for him; something had shifted inside of him, just as the tectonic plates of the earth had shifted underneath the city of San Francisco.

This is not to say that people need to give up on their marriage or quit their job and run off to Paris. Not everybody needs to have a house burn down. But the patriarchal culture that we live in and the linear way of thinking that it engenders dictates that if we go through major changes in our lives that, on paper, look like a lot of false stops and starts, or is seen to be a lack of commitment or focus, well, we've done something wrong. This is a very codependent mindset, a mindset of control. It basically says, "I'm afraid to quit my job and move to Paris, even though I really want to, so you can't either. Because if you do, I will feel threatened by that, and that's not okay. So you just stay where you are, and I will too, and we'll all continue to feel just fine, thank you very much."

When something "bad" happens, somehow we've screwed up. We did something wrong; someone is to blame. Out of our own anger and fear for survival, we will blame ourselves, or we'll blame others, or we'll do both. I'm not saying that we shouldn't take responsibility, because there is the law of cause of effect; however, the fundamental dynamics of cause and effect are so much larger and all-encompassing, and their effects are so much more profound than we perceive them to be. The butterflies flap their wings and there's a tsunami, and yet there were a thousand other factors or a million trillion other factors in addition to all those butterflies flapping their wings and the current of energy that created.

## EVERY STEP IS A PRAYER

A Native American teacher once said to me, "Every step is a prayer. When I take this step, I make this decision for seven generations forward." It meant that I need to think about what I'm doing. I need to feel into it, and I need to ask myself, "How is this going to affect those who come after me for at least seven generations?" I need to have concern, integrity, and care about what comes after me. That's part of my immortality in some way, my legacy—because who I am in the very cells of my being is going to feed and regenerate the next generation.

I'm not just me; I'm not just this body. To think that that is all I am is a very self-centered, narcissistic, egocentric way of thinking. This is skin that in seven years won't even be here because every seven years all of the cells in our body completely replace themselves; everything that you see when you look at the physical me won't be here. There will be an essential core self but nothing else. I'm beyond that; we're all beyond that, because everything is regenerating all the time.

The generations that will come after us—the animals, the plants, the trees, and every life form of the future—will be breathing the same atoms and molecules that I breathe, which are the same molecules that the dinosaurs breathed.

Nothing is being added to creation; rather, everything that exists is reformulated and presented in what appears as new forms. All the rain that we have now is the same rain from the past. People often think that we have an endless supply of resources, and even if we ran out we would find more someplace else. However, in truth, there are no *new* resources. There are *renewable* resources, but they are renewable only if we are aware that it is up to us to steward the earth in such a way that they *are* renewed.

James Martin, an English visionary who is widely considered to be an expert in the field of computers and their impact on society, is also a scholar and an author. His 1978 book, *The Wired Society,* for which he was nominated for a Pulitzer Prize, predicted the widespread use of computers and the Internet twenty-five years later, making him an acknowledged visionary as regards the future of technology. Another book of his, *Technology's Crucible,* published in 1987, contains a scenario that depicts a major attack on New York City in 1998 by Arab terrorists.

As Martin says in his book *The Meaning of the 21ˢᵗ Century,*

> The term capital refers to accumulated wealth. Human-made capital is in the form of investments, factories, cars, houses, equipment, software and so on. Natural capital refers to nature's resources: water, air, oil, minerals, natural gas, coal and living systems such as forests, grasslands, wetlands, estuaries and the oceans. . . . Natural capital is often so natural that we don't think about it, just as a fish doesn't think about the water it swims in. We don't think about what makes our air breathable, why we need insects and microbes, what the wetlands do for us or how the detergent-filled runoff from our dishwater might harm the wetlands.

He goes on to say, "Our economy is totally dependent on a depleting supply of natural capital. It is estimated that, in the last half-century, the Earth has lost a fourth of its topsoil and a third of its forest cover. We are losing fresh water at the rate of 6% per year."

Now is the time for us to become the visionary shamans. We have to become more thoughtful and heart-centered in our treatment of the earth and her resources. We must consider how we're using or abusing *this* Earth—our sacred home planet. It's very important to think about these things, and not just to think about them, but to feel into them. And even if we feel overwhelmed when we do that—a sense of "But what can I do?"—that's a good place to start.

Change is one of the biggest things that everyone needs to take responsibility for. The Aquarian visionary shaman is one who loves the earth and the imaginal realms and the cosmos as well. I recently saw a bumper sticker that said, "Green is the color of love." Green is said to be the color of the heart chakra, and it is one of the main colors that represents Gaia, the planet Earth. I feel a real resonance with green; change or transformation has definitely become my religion.

So how are we going to change? Are we going to hold on to what we have, hoard our goods and energy, and contract so small that we do not make the conscious evolutionary changes that we are here to make? If we really are "the ones we've been waiting for," we had best get on with it, we had best get on with changing our outlook, our actions, ourselves, and our relationship to the planet.

If we're the ones we've been waiting for, are we going to take responsibility for the redemption we seek? Our culture is one of celebrity, and our political system rewards this mentality. Our hoped-for candidate gets into office, and he or she doesn't deliver on what was promised on the campaign trail, so it's on to the next candidate and the next election and the next moment of holding our collective breath and praying that the change that was promised to us does in fact happen. We are so busy having elections and voting for this new hope or that new hope that we are distracted from the awareness that the power lies within.

We need to grow up from being children who have abdicated our personal responsibilities and take back our power. And we can do that. Why? Because we have the imaginal cells that are ready and waiting to inform us, to create a paradigm shift of seeing and being in the world.

Take that little acorn we see lying on the ground. If we said to it, "You see that oak tree? Well, one day you're going to *be* that oak tree," the acorn might respond in disbelief. "Oh no, I could never be that! I'm just this little acorn lying on the ground. I could never become that mighty oak tree." The answer to that is "Yes, you will, because one day in the distant past that big oak tree was just like you; it was a tiny little acorn."

And that's who *we* are too. We're just like that little acorn. The past, the present, and the future exist in who we already are. Our job is to learn how to remember that.

# 5
# THE SHAMANIC PORTAL INTO WONDERLAND

*T*o more fully understand how Shamanic Breathwork and other shamanic psychospiritual practices can guide us through a powerful portal and activate our future selves, we can look to stories that metaphorically reflect the core process of the shamanic journey. One such story is *Alice in Wonderland,* particularly the most recent movie version, directed by Tim Burton.

First of all, it's a remake, so it doesn't depict Alice as a little girl. Instead, we meet Alice as a young woman who is in the middle of accepting a proposal of marriage. She is expected to say yes. Along with this, she is expected to conform with the social norms and customs of the day.

As the story begins we are at a party in the English countryside where a very young and wealthy man named Hamish is proposing to Alice in front of many invited guests. Just at the moment that he's on bended knee in the gazebo, staring up at Alice and reciting words of love, she is distracted by the sight of a large white rabbit behind a hedge. The White Rabbit is holding a clock and hissing at her, "We're late; we're late!" For whatever reason, this resonates with Alice, and she heeds his call. She runs to the White Rabbit, leaving a puzzled Hamish in her wake. Following the rabbit, she runs through a labyrinth and then to a very old tree, which has a large hole at its base.

## FALLING DOWN THE RABBIT HOLE AND
## INTO THE IMAGINAL WORLD

We always enter the shamanic world through an imaginary portal that shape-shifts our reality; it could be a looking glass, the trunk of a tree, or a hole in a tree. Or perhaps we dive into the ocean and submerge ourselves under the waves or find ourselves climbing a spiral ladder of energy to the stars and heavenly other worlds. Some may refer to these realms as the upper, lower, and middle worlds, but in truth we may encounter countless worlds when we enter the shamanic realms.

Oftentimes our own pain brings us to our knees and opens our psyche to the realm of the imaginal worlds, where transformation and healing is possible. In Shamanic Breathwork and other processes, this can simply mean going to a quiet space and sitting, in nature or your bedroom, in the bathroom, or even on a plane. After focused breathing and going within, you allow yourself to enter the portal of surrender. You might actually visually *see* yourself moving through a portal, or you might simply sense it, but as you shape-shift through this passage, you move from one level of consciousness to another.

After Alice falls down her own shamanic portal, the hole at the base of the tree—which is also symbolic of the move from her family tree to the archetypal tree of life—and gets to the bottom of it, she is in a room with many doors. When she turns around, she sees a key sitting on a table. She tries the key in every door, but none of them opens, until she comes to the very last door. The key works and the door opens, but Alice can't fit through the doorway because she is too large! She then sees an elixir sitting on the table, and she drinks it, which makes her shrink. Finally, after all this shape-shifting, she is able to move through the open door.

We too can sometimes get "stuck" and have trouble finding our way through the cosmic birth canal while journeying from one level of consciousness to another.

Alice has had to find just the right amount of the elixir or "medicine" to make her just the right size to get through the door. Likewise, anyone attempting to undertake a shamanic journey must use the right combination of "medicine," whether it is a magical brew of a substance—such as ayahuasca or peyote or iboga—or another powerful mind-altering method. One has to learn the right formula and how to use it so that it can be an effective catalyst for change.

After Alice goes through the door, she meets all kinds of characters and beings—archetypes, if you will. We might refer to them as deities or gods of various mythologies; they include the Mad Hatter, the Cheshire Cat, the Blue Caterpillar, the Red Queen, and the White Queen.

This is all so strange to Alice, but part of it is very familiar because she has very faint memories of maybe having been in Wonderland as a child, but she doesn't know if these memories are valid, or what is real anymore. After falling down the rabbit hole, Alice thinks she's in a dream. In fact, she spends a good portion of her odyssey believing that it's *all* just a dream until she finally realizes that her experience is real and that she is awake. However, just as each character we encounter in our dreams is an aspect of our own personality, all the archetypes that Alice meets when she shape-shifts through the door are really potent aspects of herself, sent to help her undergo the transformation into her "bigger self."

In the shamanic world we would say these different aspects are her spirit guides. Some of them are shadow spirit guides, such as the Red Queen, whose consort is the Jabberwocky, a powerful dragon sort of a creature that Alice has to defeat. These are all characters in her unconscious that are, what we call from the shamanic perspective, the shadow. We also call them adversarial allies. Carl Jung, the famous Swiss psychoanalyst, defined them this way: our friends and allies support us into becoming who we are, but our adversarial allies, or our shadow, force us to become who we must! In this sense, the shadow is our friend because it brings forth our darkness so that we can turn toward the light and, in so doing, discover our true soul qualities.

This is Alice's journey, and as she continues, she encounters the Mad Hatter, who tells her that she's lost her "muchness." What does this mean, to have lost one's "muchness"? In Alice's case, it means that she's gotten too small in her outer life, with the result being that she doesn't even remember who she really is anymore.

A big debate ensues at this point, between characters who think they know her and those who insist that she really isn't the same Alice they befriended in Wonderland so long ago. This Alice is unfamiliar to them. And even though part of her experience is familiar, she agrees with them that she's not the same Alice that was there before. And of course, the truth is, she *was* there when she was a child. She loved it, and she was there frequently, and she knew them all well, but she left and doesn't fully remember being there, and she is so different now from what she was back then. But some of the characters recognize her and insist that she is Alice. The Mad Hatter, for instance, recognizes her instantly.

In the shamanic world we might say that Alice has become disconnected from her true self, her spiritual source, and that she has experienced soul loss and is in need of soul retrieval or soul return. As we mature, there is a whole way in which we lose ourselves and lose access to what we have repressed in our shadows while shrinking to fit in. In so doing, we also lose access to the spiritual realms of the imaginal world where our magic still resides. The imaginal world contains our higher self and all of our spirit guides and helpers who exist to help us in *this* world.

When the Mad Hatter tells Alice that she has lost her muchness, she doesn't quite know what he means. Later on in the story, as she is trying to make sense of everything that has happened to her, she realizes that, yes, she really *is* Alice. She has flashbacks wherein she *fully remembers* being in Wonderland as a child, when she had courage and spunk, and she used to feel joy and be feisty and fiery and very full of life.

At this point in Alice's odyssey she encounters the dragon—the consort of the evil Red Queen, who rules her kingdom with an iron fist and keeps all its peoples suppressed. Someone must fight the dragon, put down the Red Queen, and free the kingdom, and Alice knows that these challenges are hers to meet. So she dons her armor and prepares to fight.

This is the spiral path of the spiritual warrior and the path of shamanic psychospiritual transformation. When we encounter our own difficulties and dramas in life, we don our armor and we prepare, such as through Shamanic Breathwork or other modalities, to slay our dragons. We return to the Field of Plenty, and we meet our imaginal cells and embrace them through the process of breathwork in order to reclaim who we really are.

At this point Alice meets the Blue Caterpillar, who is a great master guru. He hangs upside down in a chrysalis of his own creation, smoking a hookah pipe. He is just about to complete a life cycle. Alice wants to know what's going on and the Blue Caterpillar tells her that he's finished. He is ready to change, to die, to shape-shift and morph into his next form. When Alice realizes this and sees that he has no fear around it, she is able to summon the courage and fortitude that *she* needs to face the dragon, and to possibly die in the process, to change forms herself if need be.

The Blue Caterpillar reassures her by telling her that they will meet up again, someday, somewhere. Emboldened by these words, Alice leaves him, meets the dragon on the field of battle, and after an arduous fight, slays him.

In so doing, the downfall of the evil Red Queen is brought about, and the White Queen is restored to power. Given that her task is done, Alice is ready to return to her everyday world. However, all the archetypes that she met along the way want her to stay, of course, just like Dorothy's friends want her to stay in Oz. Alice has grown very fond of these characters, just as Dorothy grew fond of the Tin Man and the Lion and the Scarecrow and Glenda the Good Witch, and even Oz himself. However, Alice *can't* stay in the archetypal world; she has to go back to the human world and manifest the changes in her outer life that have taken place within herself.

## RETURNING FROM THE IMAGINAL WORLD

None of us can stay in the imaginal world for long without losing ourselves in fantasy, disengagement, disembodiment, and dissociation. We must come back to our everyday reality of the physical world to bring meaning and relevancy to our visions. And Alice does this, but in so doing she lets them know that when she returns home she will bring the benefits of her experience in Wonderland with her. Each and every time we use our ability to go into that imaginal world and we reconnect at a deeper level to our inner shaman or higher self, we bring more of our future self and who we really are meant to be back to *this* world.

The Australian Aborigines know this. They know that the Dreamtime is as real as our physical everyday world is. To them it is very important to bring back from the Dreamtime what they learn there; otherwise, the world will become unbalanced. On our planet we've lost the natural ability to travel shamanically into the other worlds, to go into altered states, and to find the messengers from the future that can show us what we need to know now for our present-day circumstances.

When Alice comes back from the other world, she climbs out of the hole of the tree, goes back through the labyrinth, and returns to where all the people at her engagement party are waiting for her on the earth plane. Only a few seconds have elapsed there, but everything has changed. *She* has changed. She walks up to Hamish and says, "I'm sorry, Hamish. I can't marry you. You're not the right man for me. And there's that trouble with your digestion." Then she goes to her brother-in-law, who is cheating on her sister, and says, "You're lucky to have my sister for your wife, Lowell, and be good to her. I'll be watching very closely." And she walks right through them all and tells everybody, in each case, a certain truth that is unique to them that they need to hear or, even more important, that she needs to speak up about and say out loud.

She approaches Hamish's father, who was to have been her father-in-law, and announces to him that while she won't marry his son after all, she will do business with him. (Alice's own father, before he died, had been his business colleague.) Alice and Hamish's father thus become business partners, and the story ends with her sailing off to do her very first trade with the Chinese. As the ship sets sail out of the port, a blue butterfly lands on her shoulder. It is the Blue Caterpillar transformed, of course.

In this story, Alice, like the caterpillar that has turned into the butterfly, has activated her imaginal cells and has thus transformed herself from a little girl into an empowered woman. Once she has summoned the courage to meet and defeat her demons, she becomes the shamanic spiritual warrior living her true sacred purpose in the world.

## SURRENDERING TO THE MYSTERY

Alice's story is also our story. Each one of us has to learn how to fight our own dragons, how to deal with the shadow and the light, how to shape-shift, how to enter into the magical realms, how to meet our guides and our angels, and how to remember that we've done it all before. We need to learn how to remember that this is our birthright, how to remember to bring it back into this dimension of reality, and how to make it count here while we're having the human experience. Perhaps most important, we need to learn how to have the courage of our convictions to live a full and rewarding life on our soul's journey and to be of service to others along the way.

Alice's journey is one that's happening for all of us, all the time. And when each one of us decides, like the Blue Caterpillar, that it's time to become a butterfly and so we wind ourselves up in that chrysalis, we are agreeing to go into the world that we *don't* know. We are surrendering to the Great Mystery in order to transcend it. This is reflected in a quote by Einstein: "You cannot solve problems with the same level of consciousness that created them." We have to surrender and let our egos die to any presumption that makes us think we know what is really going on. Only then can we hope to one day, like the caterpillar in the chrysalis, fly as a butterfly.

# 6

# THE DIFFERENCE BETWEEN SPIRIT, SOUL, AND EGO

*What It Means to Be Fully Human*

*When you wish upon a star*
*Makes no difference who you are*
*Anything your heart desires*
*Will come to you*

LEIGH HARLINE AND
NED WASHINGTON,
"WHEN YOU WISH UPON A STAR,"
FROM WALT DISNEY'S *PINOCCHIO*

## STORIES ABOUT OURSELVES

Part of who we are as human beings consists of the story lines we have created and believe about ourselves. If enough people decide a reality is true, then it becomes consensual reality, and belief systems are formed to support those theories. People often ask, "Aren't we just making up stories about our reality?" The answer is yes, of course, but then I ask, "Why *this* reality or *this* story?" The archetypal world—the world of energetic psychic blueprints that download into our psyches—holds the big myths, and the story lines that we take on and live out in our outer lives.

The book *The Four Agreements,* written by Don Miguel Ruiz, speaks to the idea of personal story lines. It has sold approximately four million copies since publication in 1997. The Four Agreements are:

1. Be impeccable with your word.
2. Don't take anything personally.
3. Don't make assumptions.
4. Always do your best.

Don Miguel's work has often focused on dropping our story lines. While I totally understand how attached or addicted any of us can get to our story lines—such as the archetype of the victim, the hero, the bad boy, the good girl—I also believe that these story lines have a sacred purpose in that, by allowing the soul to live and move *through* them in time and space, they serve to evolve consciousness. In so doing, they allow us to love more fully, and in that, we experience higher love and wisdom.

Carl Jung taught that deep exploration into the human psyche would reveal the story lines, myths, and archetypes that are playing out, both individually and collectively, on the human stage. The Egyptian pantheon of gods and goddesses—and all of the myths that later evolved into the major religions of the world—attest to the fact that these stories are important and that they are part of the Great Mystery of being human. The Egyptians, like many ancient cultures, took great care to depict the stories of their time through countless hieroglyphic inscriptions on the walls of their temples. We see these stories and epic motifs reflected and repeated many times in later cultures through art, writing, and theater.

## CULTIVATING OUR SOUL QUALITIES

Part of this Great Mystery, I believe, is to wake up to an understanding that we are alive today to cultivate within ourselves the soul qualities learned from our life's lessons and to manifest the idea of conscious co-creation. Our life lessons are forgiveness, healing, and compassion. The myths, legends, and religions of the world contain role models for shamanic awareness: Inanna, Kuan Yin, Shakti/Shiva, White Buffalo Calf Woman, Merlin, Quetzalcoatl, Green Tara, Isis, Osiris, Demeter, Pluto, and Persephone, to name just a few. This awareness is also found in the many human spiritual leaders who have graced our presence, such as Mother Teresa, Jesus, Buddha, Mohammed, Chief Seattle, Mahatma Gandhi, and Martin Luther King Jr. These spiritual and shamanic leaders still inspire us today.

If we study the spiritual maxim "as above, so below" or Jesus's saying "on Earth as it is in Heaven," we come to understand that we can realize our shamanic psychospiritual blueprint by drawing our imaginal cells into being. "On Earth as it is in Heaven" is really a very simple prayer and invocation. I'm invoking my imaginal cells to download from the spiritual realm into my very human life so that I may manifest on Earth who I already am in the other dimension that some call Heaven.

Love has an extraordinary and very powerful quality when it is embodied in matter, a quality that is quite different than when it exists only in the invisible spiritual realm. My sense is that spirit beings have a great desire to come into form and to have a body. It is in human form that we are able to experience the joy and the pleasures of being in love—in love with people, in love with children, in love with a lover, in love with nature. Only in human form can we really worship and glorify the beauty of all of God's creation. "For thine is the kingdom and the power and the glory forever and ever. Amen."

Bringing spirit into matter is a sacred act, which is what happens when we're born. But as we mature we're apt to become cut off from spirit; all too often we become empty shells because we don't understand that our true essence is that of a spiritual being seeking to have a human experience.

Some would say that we're not capable of being fully human if we're not connected to our spirit; part of our humanity *is* about being inspirited. *Inspirited* means "to be inspired"—filled with spirit. And enthusiastic means the same thing. If we're not inspired, inspirited, enthusiastic, and happy—as the Dalai Lama spoke about—then we're most likely not living our sacred purpose in the world, and we're probably very unhappy. If the disconnect becomes too large, we may display all kinds of dysfunctional patterns. In so doing, we exacerbate our shadow. Everyone has a shadow; it's part of being human. However, it will not dominate our lives if we are humbly aware of our shortcomings and seek to know our darkness as well as our light and deal with what is preventing us from living in our fullness.

## BEYOND SPIRIT AND MATTER
## TO THE WORLD OF THE SOUL

But beyond spirit and matter, what else goes into being human? We all know the terms *heart, soul,* and *ego,* but what do they really mean, and how are they different from one another? The ego is our most human self and is deeply attached to our physical body, our emotions, and our way of thinking. While there's nothing evil or wrong about our bodies, our emotions, and our thinking, if they're not aligned with our spiritual source, we're going to be out of alignment, as we've just discussed.

What is the soul and how is it different from our spirit and our ego? Whenever I visualize the soul, I see it connected to the energy of the heart chakra, and I'm not talking about the heart simply as an organ, nor am I talking about the heart as the seat of our emotions. Soulfulness can be found in people who have openhearted chakra energy. Embodied spirits birth shamanic consciousness in their everyday living. The sacred human part of our beingness is very related to the thinking, feeling, and physical functions of our body. Spirit, on the other hand, is the whole, vast spiritual realm of energetic beings, of Great Spirit, the Great Mystery, spirit guides, and archetypes, which includes angels.

The soul is mostly related to the inner workings of the heart chakra. It could be said that the soul is at the core, or the heart of the matter.

The soul serves as a sacred filter for our experiences and gives our lives meaning and purpose. The soul knows the exact alchemical mix needed to birth a new level of consciousness in human beings. It knows how much spiritual "bigger picture" energy, how many human shadow lessons, and how much experience to allow into the mix. The soul's purpose is to remember and keep track of who we really are. The soul is the witness that remembers our journey and never forgets that it is the sacred offspring of the spirit and the human. As soon as we have reached a certain point in our human experience and we are finally ready, it asks the human ego to surrender so that our soul's purpose can be activated and awakened.

I have often referred to this in my teachings and writings as the process of Awakening the Shaman Within. When the ego says, "I can't do this anymore; this way of working is *not* working, and I'm done," the soul then says, "Good. You've gotten everything you could out of this level of awareness, and now we're going to take what you have learned and transform it into something bigger than you ever imagined it to be while you were going through it. I'm going to tell you why you just went through that experience so that it will give your journey a meaning and you will have a language to share with others."

When humans speak with words and spirit speaks through visions and the imagination, we wonder how our ego can actually communicate with spirit in a meaningful way. The answer is that *they communicate through the soul*. The soul can read the symbolic hieroglyphs of the spirit; it connects the symbols of the spirit with the emotions, thoughts, and utterances of the human, and in so doing, translates the true meaning and purpose of our lives. If we don't have a significant reason to be alive and feel the value thereof, then we're probably out getting drunk, sleeping with the neighbor's husband or wife, or acting out in some other dysfunctional behavior.

Thus the soul is the intermediary between the ego and the spirit. The soul is also sometimes referred to as the Holy Spirit, the Christed one, or the Buddha mind. The truly open heart might also be called the bodhisattva of compassion, the shamanic bridge that connects soul, ego, and spirit. It's the intercessor, and as such, the truly open heart knows that it is part spirit and part human and that it functions as the rainbow bridge connecting the seven chakras. Sometimes in shamanism, a shaman is referred to as a "spirit lawyer." That's because the shaman knows how to negotiate and mediate between the different levels of consciousness—between the human, soul, and spiritual realms. Shamanic work involves engaging and healing all the chakras and the human heart, which must be involved for returning lost soul parts.

When someone experiences too much soul loss, that person loses the ability to experience the healing energies of love and loses the direct pipeline to his or her spiritual source. When this happens, the individual is oriented toward life with the ego only and loses the connection with the soul and the spirit. When shamans seek to heal soul loss, it's in order to return the individual to a fully functioning state—a state in which soul, spirit, and ego are fully and equally engaged and integrated.

Now remember, our human existence is in the realm of matter, and spirit lives beyond form and seeks to embody form from its imaginal realms. But the soul travels through space and time and exists in both worlds at once. That's why it's considered to be a walker between worlds—the shaman. If we wish to engage our spiritual counterparts and our imaginal cells, which include our spirit guides, helpers, angels, and animal totems, and if we want to access the spirit of Jesus Christ, the Buddha mind, the bodhisattva of compassion, and Kuan Yin, if we want to tap in to the mother goddess Isis or the great Madonna, we have to be able to lift up the energies of our humanity to meet the energies that are coming downward from spirit—and the place where they meet is upon the altar of the heart.

The Bible says, "Wherever your heart is, there your treasure will be also." The heart is the soul of the world, so if we've lost a deep connection to our heart, we also feel the loss of our soul.

When we're out of touch with our heart, we are uncaring, apathetic, and oftentimes complacent. We may find ourselves drifting through each day, doing the minimum necessary to make a living, to eat, to maintain relationships, and to take care of the kids. We can't even really focus on the present, let alone the future.

But if our *spirits* are engaged with our human self, we come to understand that we're not only human, we are so much more than that! We come to understand that the human life, while sacred and significant, is really just a blip on our soul's radar screen when compared with the much larger eternity of who we really are.

In any culture, the way to defeat a race of people is to take away what has spiritual value for them, their gods. That's all you have to do. You don't have to kill them, and you don't have to shackle them; just take away their gods and you'll defeat them. It is said that St. Patrick ran the snakes out of Ireland. In actual fact, he ran out the Druids, the exalted elders of the pagan religion; Ireland is now a very Christian country.

The Catholic Church's use of the Latin liturgy long after the language was in common use provides another example. The common people, not understanding what was being said, had to rely on the priests for interpretation. As long as you can keep people ignorant of the means by which they may access their own spiritual connection and they have to go through a priest or a guru to find God, you can control them, for their relationship to spirit is only halfhearted. However, if people have a direct connection to spirit, their hearts are engaged. They are empowered, and you can't defeat them.

## ETOWAH, THE SPIRIT OF THE FUTURE

Recently I had a lucid dream vision in which I saw an energy form rising up out of a smoky mist. It wasn't the energy of a human person;

it was more like a spirit of some kind. I couldn't really see clearly, through the mist, what the form actually was, but it did tell me its name was Etowah. This spirit of Etowah conveyed many wondrous things to me. It said that whenever we ask for something, whether we ask consciously or unconsciously in our hidden thoughts, we are invoking a powerful prayer. Every thought—whether it's conscious or unconscious—is a prayer.

Etowah conveyed to me, not in words, but in thought-forms, "I am that which answers your prayers. I am an energy that has no choice except to answer your prayers. I am your loyal servant. I am the delivery system between your prayer and the source of the Field of Plenty from which all prayers are answered. I am the conduit. I am the mist between the worlds, and I have no choice. I have no discernment; I have no voice in the matter. My sole function is to answer all beings' prayers, and they are answered from the point of consciousness from which they are asked—be it high, low, good, bad, evil, or righteous—because in this form, the light and the dark are no different. It's all just energy, and it's up to human beings to differentiate, because beyond the fact that form simply exists, there is no real good or bad, right or wrong, evil or righteousness, in the bigger picture."

We, as humans, assign right and wrong, good and evil, happiness and sadness. But in the world beyond right and wrong, the world of spirit, these things are undifferentiated. And while there are archetypes of low-density consciousness that are known in our world as evil, which individuals embody sometimes unconsciously or unknowingly because of their wounded egos, in the world of spirit, there is no such distinction.

To illustrate how unconditional and unattached the world of pure spirit is, I want to tell you about another dream, one that a good friend of mine had. Her dream has everything to do with the soul, the spirit, and the human part of us. She is a high-powered corporate business professional in the banking world who has been feeling stuck in a relationship for quite a while. She is in love with a man who does not meet her needs, and she can't decide whether she should, or even can, end the relationship.

Recently, she had a highly charged dream, and she asked me to help her interpret it because she didn't have any idea what it meant.

In it, she was very high up on a mountaintop, where there lived a tribe of native people. It was a rather otherworldly place, and she didn't glean a lot about them except that they were very wise. My friend wanted to go up there. She also knew that a woman had journeyed to that place to be with this tribe and had actually fallen in love with a male member of the clan. The woman had stayed there and become part of their culture, similar to the movie *Avatar* when Sigourney Weaver integrated with the tribespeople.

So my friend, the woman having the dream, wanted to go to this otherworldly realm, but it was almost straight up, like a cliff. Because of this, she had no idea how she was supposed to get up there, when suddenly a car appeared and she realized that someone was in the driver's seat, but she never saw who it was. The driver drove the car straight up the mountain, which totally blew my friend away.

It was like going up a roller coaster. It slowly made its way up, and when it got to the very top, there was a little hole in the mountain where the tires could lodge so the car wouldn't roll back down. Someone who had learned how to walk on such a steep slope walked down from the top of the mountain and opened the car door to greet her.

This person said, "Take my hand, and walk this way, and lean that way, and you'll get the hang of it." And they walked up to the top where the tribe was. My friend met them all and really connected with them. At the same time, she realized that not very far above her head, so close that she might be able to touch it, was the ceiling of the world, the very top of the world.

The people at the top of the world were very spiritual; they barely needed to take a breath because of their essence and their energy. She asked the woman who had moved there from below, "How do you do things up here? It seems like everything is so difficult, given the steepness of the terrain and the fact that you don't really breathe." And then, knowing that a man was the reason why this woman was up there, she said, "How, for instance, do you make love?"

The other woman proceeded to explain that she and her male partner couldn't actually have sex that high up, that if they did their hearts would burst. So instead, if people met up there and fell in love, they would make their way back down the mountain together to a place where they were able to get married, make love, sire children, and have normal, everyday lives. Then later, when they had lived those lives out on the physical plane, they would make their journey back up to the top of the mountain. From there they could look out over everything, and as a result, they knew what was going on: they knew the answers to everything; it was the source of their great wisdom.

My friend was amazed at this, and she took advantage of the opportunity to ask these people about her relationship dilemma. She said to them, "I need to ask you whether I should stay with this man I am in love with. My needs aren't getting met, but I can't seem to find the strength to break off the relationship. What should I do?"

They just looked at her with incredulous expressions and then smiled. She said, "Can't you please tell me? You're supposed to know everything." Do you know what they said to her? They said, "Well, we could tell you, but it's not really important." "What do you mean?" she asked them. They said, "From up here, it doesn't matter what you do. It's all about learning from life. It doesn't really matter to your spirit either. It's just your human journey. Whatever decisions you make, you make!"

She lived her life obsessing about these things that, at a higher level, were not important at all. This had become an addictive pattern for her, and while it seemed pretty important to the *human* part of who she was, in the larger context, it was insignificant. It was just another experience, neither right nor wrong, neither good nor bad. It was what it was.

My friend asked me what the whole dream meant. I laughed and said, "I feel like you have just described the journey of the ego, the soul, and the spirit. The base of the mountain is the equivalent of our lower chakras, and when we live there, and get a glimpse of heaven, or the top of the world, if you will, we cannot envision how we could ever live there and survive. We look up there and say, 'The way is too steep; this is just too hard; I can never get there.'

"But then all of a sudden a car shows up, with a driver aboard. I think that this driver is really the soul, which mediates between the human part of ourselves and the spiritual part of ourselves, which puts us in the vehicle and 'drives' our spiritual hunger to the top of the mountain, where it can be fulfilled. You're amazed and somewhat scared, but you also feel very trusting that some part of yourself can take you to this height. It's so high that it's like your crown chakra; it's at the very top of the ceiling, and you can touch it.

"When you get there, your higher self, your spiritual self, greets you and explains what it's like to be a spiritual being and how the questions that we obsess about in human form aren't really that important after all. Your spiritual self will also tell you that if you want to have a human life, you have to go back down the mountain and do the things that people do: make love, eat, build a house, maybe have some kids or get a job.

"There's nothing wrong with being in the lower realm. In fact, all the beings who are in the higher realm go back down to the lower realm to do normal human things. This is such a perfect example of these three parts of ourselves: the spirit knowing what happens in the lower realm; the human ego wanting to understand the spiritual life; and the soul saying, 'I can take you safely up and down.'"

By doing this, by traveling from the lower realm to the upper realm and back again, we navigate from one world to the other, just like the being who met my friend up at the higher realm and, after helping her from the car, said, "After you walk around here for a while you'll get the hang of it." We are walkers between the worlds, and that means that we are spiritual beings having a human experience. One of the ways we are able to do that is by being able to navigate between the worlds.

If we stay only in one realm or the other, we tend to get polarized, either in the light or the dark, and we don't have the full experience of what it means to be spiritualized humans. We lose part of our essence when it's difficult, and we're struggling with an issue, and we get into all of our emotions and all of our judgments. It's fine to have emotions, but it's really difficult when they have us.

To have emotions is like having a car. But a car doesn't have you; you have the car. Sometimes we get lost on our path, and we give our power away to our emotions and to our thoughts. It's great to have thoughts, but when our thoughts overtake us and we become obsessed and have compulsions, we're no longer in power. It's great to have a body, but what if you get paralyzed from the neck down, and you're like Stephen Hawking, who uses a speech synthesizer? His body doesn't have him; he has his body. It's been said that the garden of the soul is the body. But it's important to remember that the body is pretty lonely without the spirit. Our spirit can exist without our ego and our human self; however, to have the magnificent experience of being human, the spirit does need a body with thoughts and emotions.

When these people said to my friend, "I know these questions are very important to the human part of you, but at the highest level they really don't matter. You're here to do your human thing and learn what you need to learn, and whatever you're doing is neither right nor wrong; it's just what it is," that was very difficult for her ego to hear.

It's very difficult for the emotional, intellectual, physical part of us, because we are always trying to quantify everything we do and assign it a meaning. It's not very easy to hear that if people are murdered it's okay, or if a certain species becomes extinct it's all right, or if the polar ice caps melt it's really no big deal. At the same time, the other side of that coin is that spirits would not have become human if they did not want to have difficult earthly experiences as well as joyful ones.

Spirit beings who want to have a human experience do need an Earth plane, a material plane, on which to be and to have experiences. Earth is a very valuable place to spirit; it is a university of sorts. It's as if spirit said, "Where can I go in the universe where I will have the opportunity to really, really evolve?" It found Earth, or it created Earth.

Spirit needed a planet that consisted of both shadow and light so that it could have a really intense experience of the unity, the duality, and the trinity. Earth is a place where I get the opportunity, within the duality, to remember my wholeness, my oneness, where I get the opportunity to go all the way to the dark side and die and then go all the way to the light and be reborn, in every breath I take, in every inhale and exhale of my various physical incarnations and experiences—be they happy or sad or joyful or tragic.

So how does that tie in to our larger discussion and what Etowah conveyed to me?

In *my* dream, Etowah said, "I am the spirit; I am the energy of the future that is the delivery system of what you have prayed for, consciously or unconsciously, and I must deliver from the One Source, from the Uniworld, from the Field of Plenty, what you have asked for. I have no other directive; it's what I do, and it's my sacred function. I have no judgment about what I bring to you or even what you ask for; I am just the messenger."

Could this spirit that showed up in my dream actually have been the archetypal energy of fate? What is fate exactly? Whenever I hear anyone talk about being lucky, I frequently reply that I don't believe in luck. I believe that everything has a purpose and that we're not lucky or unlucky. I may say I am very fortunate, but not lucky. Luck indicates that something happens by accident, and I don't believe in accidents. I do believe that things happen through fate and that fate is the inevitable conclusion of the energy that we draw to ourselves by our actions, our thoughts, our emotions, and our being.

This message from Etowah was very powerful. Etowah said, "Whatever you bring in to your life, whether you acknowledge it as your prayers answered or not, will begin to shape-shift your consciousness through your experiences. And as it shape-shifts that consciousness, your outer world will be reinvented over and over again."

Etowah said, "Please know that whatever a man or a woman thinks in their hearts there also is their treasure; that's where their home is," which reflects the quote I used at the beginning of this chapter. It means coming home to the hidden power of holy longing, pure discernment, and the true love that's hidden within every human heart.

It's up to the human heart to make the distinction about what is worthy and what is not, about what to do when our prayers are answered and we are trying to figure out our next right step. If I win the lottery, am I going to reinvest all of my newly acquired wealth in the stock market, hoping to increase it for my own personal aggrandizement? Or will I invest some and also set up a charitable foundation to help feed the hungry of the world? I look to my heart to tell me what to do.

When we bring in the discerning power of the human heart, we really begin to realize that we create our reality and that our fate is in our own hands, because the heart further refines what is presented to us through our answered prayers. The heart is a great filter that some traditions have even referred to as the true Holy Grail; it knows how to hold all that we are and transmute the dross of our being into pure gold.

The onus is on us as human beings to take real responsibility for all our actions, instead of leaving it up to an outside source to fix everything that we feel is wrong with the world today. All humans must use their untapped powers of the heart—not to be overly sentimental or overly emotional, but to embrace our intellectual powers, reasoning abilities, and emotional intelligence. We must also embrace our deep instincts and intuition, and rise above intellectualism and emotionalism to find the bigger picture of our prayers. We must learn to consciously think with our hearts to ensure that we are standing in real integrity and coming from a heart-centered place and not from the ego.

## SURRENDERING THE HUMAN HEART

When I awoke from this dream about Etowah, I lay thinking about it for a little while, and then I recalled a dream I had when I was twenty-one or twenty-two, which was a mixture of an out-of-body experience and a lucid dream. It had to do with a powerful scene in which I surrendered my heart in a ritual for a higher purpose.

In this dream I was a fourteen- or fifteen-year-old girl wearing a gleaming white robe, which signified that I was some sort of an initiate. I was walking out on cliffs that were very high and that overlooked a desert or a valley. Trees were below, and the ground cover was sand, and while it was reminiscent of Egypt, I remember thinking that it might actually be the legendary Atlantis.

My dream progressed, and I stepped out of a cave that contained a lot of other male and female initiates. Together we walked across a long bridge made of gold. I sensed we had all been raised in a temple specifically for this ritual, and after crossing the bridge, we walked through an opening in stone into a huge pyramid. Inside were priests and priestesses dressed in elaborate costumes of white and gold. In the center of the pyramid was a big slab of stone, an altar of some kind. It was all rather magnificent, with dancing light reflecting off embedded crystals in the walls.

Each of us walked slowly and ceremonially up to the altar one at a time. Once there, the priests and priestesses helped us onto the slab. Then they cut into us and took out our hearts, and in so doing we silently died. Because I knew this was going to happen, I felt a little scared, but then again I had been raised for this purpose and was equally happy and excited. As awful as this ritual might sound to some, it did not feel evil to me in the dream body at all. I somehow knew that my beating heart, once it was removed from my body, would be used to keep the planet in balance; it was a necessary sacrifice. It all felt as if it was part of something that I had agreed to prior to my coming to the planet.

Before I was laid on the slab, I was asked, "Are you ready to surrender your heart, Y'tawah?" Since the time that I had this dream, I've tried to find the meaning of this word Y'tawah, but to no avail. Y'tawah sounds a lot like Etowah, the spirit in my dream. The name of the goddess Kuan Yin also sounds like it could be a form of Y'tawah. Of course, Kuan Yin has a compassionate heart, and she is the one who embraces her emotions, integrates them with her intellect, and thus becomes the bodhisattva of compassion.

Perhaps Y'tawah wasn't just my name in the dream. Perhaps it is a name given or bestowed on each person who willingly walks forward to surrender his or her heart. Maybe it's everyone's initiation for the healing and expanding of the heart as we move from ego to our true soul nature.

I don't know the full answers to these questions, but I do know that this spirit, this energy form, Etowah, has grabbed me completely and has said to me, "If you want to learn from the future and create your own destiny, you must consciously, truly go past your ego mind and your emotions into your heart's secret longing; there you must listen with your heart and your mind. Breathe and keep breathing, opening, and listening for the energies of your potential future self. Look into the future, and see the myriad possibilities. Select the one that is the best fit for who you are here to be and for your special role on the planet at this time."

We are all already doing this at some level, but often we're doing it more or less unconsciously. It's a matter of making it conscious, of thinking consciously with the heart. In ancient Egypt they used to take out various organs, put them into canopic jars,* and save them for the afterlife. The brain was not considered valuable; some mythologists claim they threw it into the Nile where it was eaten by crocodiles. Ancient Egyptians believed that inner knowing and wisdom came through and was centered in the heart.

It is the heart that *needs to decide* what is going to be allowed to come into manifestation. It is in this heart-place—a place that filters out our judgments from the ego, that filters out fears from childhood, that filters out our anxieties and our phobias and our hang-ups—that pure knowing is found.

---

*Canopic jars are also known as funerary jars; they were meant to hold certain internal organs of the deceased. These jars (usually numbering four) were found in ancient tombs. They stored organs that were believed to be essential for the dead person's existence in the afterlife.

# 7

# SHAPE-SHIFTING THE FAMILY TREE INTO THE COSMIC TREE OF LIFE

*O*ur family of origin makes up our family tree, and all the issues that come up around our family of origin rightfully belong to our past. However, our past is a living reality. It has its own energetic dimension, its own realm of existence that is still out there living in its own world. It has its own energy, if you will, composed of archetypes and forms that continue to have a powerful hold and influence over our identity unless we pay close attention and do our best to heal it.

Clearing our patterns is analogous to a property that you've just bought with a lot of fallen trees and debris. If you have a large piece of property, you could be clearing those trees for years. You think you've done a lot of work, but one day you look up and notice how much more work there is to be done.

While it's also true that even though we may do a lot of work to clear our patterns, sometimes it's difficult to clear them completely. The most important thing to realize is that, while some of the patterns may remain, in one form or another, it's key not to allow ourselves to be *triggered* by them when someone or something pushes our buttons. Instead of automatically defaulting to our prior reactive behavior, it's important to stop, take a breath, and respond in the appropriate fashion to the disrupting action or event.

When we conduct our family of origin initiation in our healing programs at Venus Rising, we speak about the family as the gift that keeps on giving. Ha! A friend of mine has a plaque outside his door that reads, "Friends always welcome; family by appointment." If you're laughing at this, then you know what I'm talking about. You're probably one of the walking wounded. But all kidding aside, the point is, we *can* heal our wounds. When we gain enough consciousness around them and know they're there, we won't automatically default to them in times of stress or struggle or fear.

That's a sign of great progress, and it can be incredibly transformative for people to realize. Also, the further away we get from the behaviors and dysfunctional patterns in our lives that activate our triggers, the less frequently they will arise in the future.

## THE GIFTS OF THE FAMILY TREE

It's important to identify our issues and triggers. They really do come from the family of origin tree, the family tree, if you will. We may hear the words *family tree* and wonder what this phrase really means. Most of us immediately think about genealogy, our grandparents and great-grandparents. Perhaps we trace our family lineage back a generation or two or three or four. If you're a real genealogy whiz, you might trace your lineage back to find out what boat your family crossed the ocean on, or who the famous members of your family may have been, or its villains and heroes.

Often, in the family of origin work that I do with people, and especially in the area of addiction, we look at the family lineage and draw lines connecting the generational issues. Even if you didn't personally know your great-grandma or great-grandpa, for instance, we might look for certain information, such as a great-grandma who was schizophrenic or a great-grandpa who was alcoholic. We might discover that there were suicides in three generations. Then we look at the person who we are working with to see if they have some of those same issues or patterns.

We can see somebody's personal characteristics and say, "Oh, you look like your mother" or "You laugh like your father." We might see the way somebody gestures or walks and remark on how similar it is to an ancestor or relative of theirs. Even if the person never knew his or her ancestor, these things get passed down biochemically, as memory in the genetic code. They can also be passed down from learning, from mimicking, as well as from the unconscious signals that we pass on to future generations.

It's important to realize that all of humanity is from the same original family tree. Even if you say the lineages are divided into yellow, white, red, and black, many of the research evolutionists say that we all came from Africa, and if you take it as far back as it can go, one of the prevailing evolutionary theories of today is that the very first race was black.

In that one family tree from which we all derive, only a certain amount of themes can be played out, but they are played out repeatedly. That's why we can all relate to each other if we get honest and talk about our real problems and issues.

We might try to argue with that by saying, "This person is a murderer; this person is a rapist; this person is a womanizer; this person is honorable; and this person is efficient or brilliant or talented or gifted." However, we all share these same themes in the mix whether we take on a specific role or not. Addictionologists and psychologists identify four major archetypal roles that children appropriate: the hero, the scapegoat, the lost child, or the mascot. Or they may choose a combination of those roles.

Now let's look at the tree itself and its basic symbolism. When we study it closely, we realize that the tree is a very important symbol in almost every spiritual culture. In the Jewish tradition we have the

Kabbalah.* Kabbalists believe the Tree of Life is a representation of how the universe was manifested at the beginning of time. However, the Tree of Life also symbolizes humanity's place in the universe, with the consciousness of humankind being a fruit of the physical world through which spirit is continuously expressed.

According to the Kabbalist view, matter was originally formed from spirit, and now matter (which includes humans) seeks to reunite with its true nature by learning to know itself again. Humankind seeks to regain knowledge of its divine identity by stages that make up the Sephiroth.† We travel back up the Tree of Life until this union, or reunion, is complete.

Gnostic Christianity has a motif that is similar to the Kabbalistic Tree of Life. Called the Pleroma, it represents the constant, variably nuanced emanations from God, which *is* God. These emanations increase in complexity the closer they are to the original creative source. The last emanation in the Pleroma is named Sophia, which corresponds to the final Sephirah on the Kabbalistic Tree of Life, named Keter.

The Hindu religion has the Asvattha, the Tree of Life and Being, which is a bit anomalous in that it is said to have its branches on the ground and its roots in the air. The ground represents the world; the roots in the air are in God; the leaves of the tree symbolize the Vedas.‡ In Christianity we have the tree in the Garden of Eden, which bears the fruit of good and evil. We also have the tree that became the wooden cross that Christ was crucified on in order to bear the sins of the world, redeem human beings, and spiritualize matter. This is known as the Tree of the Cross.

There is also the World Tree, Yggdrasil, which Odin hung from

---

*Kabbalah is the mystical esoteric discipline of Rabbinic Judaism, which seeks to determine the relationship between God and His created universe and to answer ontological questions concerning the the meaning of existence.

†Sephiroth are the ten manifestations of God in the Jewish tradition of the Kabbalah.

‡The Vedas are the four basic texts that comprise the fundamentals of Hinduism: the Rig Veda, Sama Veda, Yajur Veda, and Atharva Veda. The oldest one, the Rig Veda, was created in the second century BCE.

upside down for nine days before discovering the symbols of the sacred runes of divination and magic. The runes would help to give him authority and empower him in the nine worlds of Norse cosmology. The Buddha sat under the Bodhi Tree until he gained enlightenment. In pagan belief systems, the ancient Druids worshipped in open clearings surrounded by oak groves. The symbolism goes on and on.

The family of origin tree is a symbolic connection linking us to our very human lineage and ancestors. This tree comprises the roots of our human family and tells us, among other things, where we've come from, how we've grown, and how we've branched out into becoming the different races of the earth, which are called root races. The tree, as a symbol, solidifies our agreement to be here and to be human beings going through the cycles of death and rebirth, the cycles of change and growth.

The problem arises when we forget the mystery, when we forget that there is another greater type of tree, which is the Tree of Life, also known as the World Tree. This Tree of Life is different than the family tree. This Tree of Life is much bigger than our mere humanity, and it didn't begin here on Earth. This archetypal Tree of Life is being downloaded all the time. This Tree of Life is an eternal tree, it's the life-force energy—it's the Tree of Consciousness itself.

It's said that if we look closely at a human brain, it resembles a tree, with all the circuitry that goes through it symbolized by the branches, the trunk, and the roots. Perhaps at some level the great mystical Tree of Life is linked to the mind of God. This Tree of Life is the thinking, feeling, life-force energy that we all come from and that we all return to when we cease being human. The archetypes or our oversouls, if you want to call them that, are formed in this very special place.

Recently I read an account of a man, Mellen-Thomas Benedict, who died from cancer,* and after an hour and a half of being clinically "dead," he came back into a healthy body that was cancer-free. During the time that he was "dead," his soul traveled to the farthest reaches of

---

*Please see www.mellen-thomas.com for more information on Benedict's riveting experience.

the galaxy and beyond, and he was given many insights into the nature of reality, some of which I will refer to here. He discusses a matrix of consciousness that he was made aware of, wherein every human being is connected to every other human being, and also connected directly to the source.

> We all have a higher Self, or an oversoul part of our being. It revealed itself to me in its truest energy form. The only way I can really describe it is that the being of the higher Self is more like a conduit. It did not look like that, but it is a direct connection to the Source that each and every one of us has. We are directly connected to the Source. . . . We have a grid around the planet where all the higher Selves are connected. This is like a great company, a next subtle level of energy around us, the spirit level, you might say. . . . Then the Light turned into the most beautiful thing that I have ever seen: a mandala of human souls on this planet. Now I came to this with my negative view of what was happening on the planet. So as I asked the Light to keep clarifying for me, I saw in this magnificent mandala how beautiful we all are in our essence, our core. We are the most beautiful creations. The human soul, the human matrix that we all make together is absolutely fantastic, elegant, exotic, everything. I just cannot say enough about how it changed my opinion of human beings in that instant. I said, "Oh, God, I did not know how beautiful we are."

I think this is an apt summation of what I deem to be the Tree of Life. Another way to think of it, or perhaps it's really the same way, is to know that our ancestors and our parents are the divine thoughts of God. We, then, become the *fruits* of the divine thoughts of God. These powerful emanations or rays or vibrations or impulses of the Tree of Life have brought forth and manifested the *fruit* of life in a condensed form. You might think of the sap or the juice or the flow of life running through the tree and out its branches into form; I believe that we human beings *are* those forms.

As Mellen-Thomas says above, through the matrix of our higher selves, we are all connected to the source of everything that is—the very heart and mind of God. We can tap directly into that source when we use methodologies such as Shamanic Breathwork or meditation. We can tap in to the source when we do yogic postures that remind us of our wholeness; or perform mudras* or chants or trance-dance; or take part in a sweat lodge ceremony. In that direct place of source, when we connect with it, we receive greater recollections of who we really are. In so doing, this makes our family of origin tree so much smaller, thereby allowing it to be in its proper, proportionate place in our lives.

A shift in our consciousness happens when we see this. That shift says, "Why am I making such a big deal out of this particular little thing, or why am I having such an exaggerated response to what so and so just said, or why am I feeling like such a victim at the hands of my parents or my partner or my daughter or my kids or my employer? Why am I letting any one thing effect me so hugely when it's really so small and insignificant in comparison with this One World, this Uniworld, where everything comes from, where everything is truly possible? Why do I allow what's happened in my life or my family's life to control me so completely?"

## SHIFTING FROM THE FAMILY OF ORIGIN TREE TO THE TREE OF LIFE

This has been a big part of the teaching that I've been bringing forth in my own life lately: we are all collectively beginning to make a conscious shift from the family of origin tree to the true Tree of Life. This is the real task facing us all. If we can honor our family of origin for what it is, and know that we have chosen our particular family in order to undergo a specific set of experiences to grow as spiritual beings and thereby advance consciousness, we can let go of its hold on us and focus

---

*A mudra is a positioning of the hands to guide energy and achieve a desired intention.

instead on the larger tree of life, which is comprised of all of humanity.

We have all chosen different things to experience because we thought we were up to those particular tasks. We have made these choices not only to experience challenges but also to experience the beauty of this place and to honor creation. At the same time, we absolutely must remember that this is not all there is; there is so much more—we're not limited to just this planet and just this consciousness.

When we can honor the understanding that we have chosen our particular families to learn the lessons we are learning, or that we have chosen this human and very sacred experience to go through, we become more Godlike and truly step into our divinity. This was the original intention of how we were meant to be on Earth, as represented by the Garden of Eden, wherein we were given the sacred responsibility to be the caretakers of this planet. We weren't given all of our resources to use up; we were asked to become shepherds, to become stewards of the earth, and to develop our human consciousness so that we could take on that divine role here.

I've spoken of this before. I feel that the mineral, animal, and plant kingdoms have all done their jobs in that they have all entered in to their own divinity. Now it's our turn; it's time for humanity to find its own divinity in right relationship to everything else.

The rocks and the trees and the rivers and the mountains have already learned this. The plants know how to support each other. The trees in the forest know when to die out to allow other types of trees to come in. They've learned how to ebb and flow, how to be dominant and then recessive, how to sacrifice themselves when they need to and how to go for the greatest good of the whole rather than just pure individual success. They do this because they know we are all one, which we humans have yet to learn.

We're also here to learn about unconditional love. We're here to really learn about the evolution of that process and to embrace the bigger picture of consciousness emerging. There have been times in history when it was very important to learn this, but if there was ever a time that it was relevant, it certainly is now, when we have the capability of blowing each other up and ending this great human experiment once and for all. I believe with our whole being that this is the largest role we have to play, but if we're not doing the work and we are remaining in our patterns, we're going to stay mired in the past. It is time to live our future in the present and let our past spin itself out. We need visit our past only when there's a lesson to learn. It's a waste of our precious life-force energy when we hang out in our personal history most of the time.

Having said all that, I believe it's important to have a sense of compassion for our humanity and how quickly we can be drawn into something, and to acknowledge what a huge act of courage it is to feel our feelings and be human and then to do the work, the deep personal work that it takes to overcome those lesser gods of addiction and distraction and codependency. It takes such a huge effort, and yet when we do it, we're so rewarded and so expanded, and consciousness in general expands around us too.

## ANUBIS AND THE TREE OF LIFE

In *The Anubis Oracle** deck there is an initiatory card that shows Anubis wrapped up in a mummy wrap hanging upside down from the Tree of Life. Standing next to him is Bast, his consort, who appeared to me as a black panther. Bast's energy is that of holy longing, rebirthing, sexuality, and desire. On the tree are luscious fruits, and Thoth, in one of his emanations as a serpent, is at the top of the tree, holding the feet of Anubis and connecting him to the tree.

Anubis hangs upside down with his eyes closed in a very reflective pose that looks so much like the caterpillar who has woven himself into

*The Anubis Oracle* is a book and deck of cards created by Linda Star Wolf, Nicki Scully, and Kris Waldherr. It is designed to be a guide to Inner Egypt and the shamanic mysteries of Egypt that live within us. The full-color deck contains a Key Card, cards for twenty-two deities and four elements, and eight composite cards that portray several deities together representing eight major portals of initiation and complex archetypal relationships.

*The Tree of Life: Bast, Anubis, and Osiris*
*(Illustration ©2011 by Kris Waldherr, www.KrisWaldherr.com)*

the chrysalis. Floating beneath Anubis, in the Nile River, is Lord Osiris, Anubis's father, who is the sacred archetype and principle of death, regeneration, and transmutation.

I can't help but go back to this card over and over again, to glean what it really means. What it means to me now is so much more than what it meant to me initially because I've spent a lot of time with it and I've delved into its mysteries to a greater extent over the years. It continues to instruct me: "In order to become Anubis, the enlightened visionary heart shaman, we must surrender."

But what is it that we must surrender? Once again, it seems that the heart is the only real treasure that is worth giving up to the gods. Bast stands beside Anubis, and we know she represents holy longing for regeneration. Thus, the message seems clear: If you want to satisfy your holy longing, you're going to have to go into the cocooned place of the chrysalis, and you're going to have to dissolve yourself so that a new wisdom can come in. That's what Thoth represents, communication and inner wisdom. Thoth also represents enlightenment, so if you want to be enlightened, you're going to have to be willing to basically turn things upside down. You have to turn your life upside down and hang upside down on that family tree in order to gain a different perspective, one other than the one you've been living your life through. You must do this to step into your own divinity and start being sustained by the larger Tree of Life.

It's like the hanged man in the tarot. You've really got to turn yourself around and see things completely differently. With the new eyes of seeing, you realize that you must surrender all the old stuff you've been struggling with. You know that it has been part of your learning process, but by staying trapped by the old stuff you will not be able to embrace the principle of Bast. Your holy longing will not be satisfied, and you will not be born into who you really are meant to be.

Anubis, in the Tree of Life, is very much like Christ or Odin. At the exact right moment, he knows that he's going to be enlightened. He knows that he will drop into the water to meet Osiris, his father, and regenerate to another level of enlightenment.

In this case, Osiris is not only his father on Earth; he's also his father in the Duat, in the other world. We can even say, "On Earth as it is in Heaven" because Osiris is *in* the other world. When Anubis goes into that deep place, when he falls into the water, into the primordial soup, if you will, and meets his father, it's like meeting God. When he meets that energy he sees and knows *everything*—he knows his humanity, his quest, and his responsibility. He becomes the walker between the worlds, and that provides the initiation he requires to become the shaman and the opener of the way for others.

So, truthfully, when we engage in the Tree of Life initiation, when we make that leap from the family of origin tree to the greater, larger, more cosmic Tree of Life, we shift from the everyday ordinary consciousness of our caterpillar self into our butterfly self. This shift is a divine gift, enabling us to remember who we really are. In so doing, we become walkers between worlds. We realize that we're spiritual humans and that we're here to have a human experience, but we now view that experience in a different way. We are, as Christ said, "In the world, but not of it." We know that this is not our final resting place, nor the final resting place of our true, highest self.

This particular mystery is one that we can all contemplate by working with *The Anubis Oracle* or with the archetypes. I do a Tree of Life reading wherein I draw four cards from the deck: one for Anubis, one for the tree, one for Bast, and one for Osiris. These cards tell me what one is dying to, surrendering to, letting go of, and really longing to become.

As we have seen with Anubis, when he finishes his initiation, he is no longer just Anubis; he is a visionary shaman. And this is true for all of us. When we face what we're really longing for and what we have to let go of in order to acquire it, and then we surrender to that, we become the Christed one. When we are initiated from the family tree into the Tree of Life, we learn to truly walk between the worlds of spirit and everyday existence, and we come to understand what it means to be fully human on this planet at this very pivotal time in our collective history.

# 8

# Direct Encounters with the Neteru of Egypt

*Re-creating the Ka Body*

*I*n the preceding chapter I touch on the spiral path of transformation and discuss some of the Egyptian gods and goddesses who assist us on that journey. Prior to my trip to Egypt in 2005 with my husband, Brad, I was not very familiar with any of these archetypal deities. The way I made their acquaintance is a very interesting story in and of itself.

## PASSAGEWAY TO EGYPT

When Brad and I first decided to visit Egypt, we were following up on a relationship we had developed with Nicki Scully when we were living in Marin County, California. Nicki is a very gifted alchemical shamanic teacher and healer who also focuses on working with the transformative power of the Egyptian mysteries. In 1978, she traveled to Egypt with the Grateful Dead, who performed concerts in front of the Sphinx and the pyramids. Since that time, Nicki has developed a long and intimate history with that country and travels there often, leading groups on special mystical journeys.

Nicki and I originally connected with one another through our newsletters and really liked each other's writing; our friendship developed from that. Because I felt drawn to her and wanted to meet her in person, Brad and I ended up going up to Eugene, Oregon, where Nicki lives and offers workshops, on our way to teach one of our own workshops near Portland, Oregon, in the summer of 2002.

We met Nicki and had a powerful experience with her in her healing and teaching center. About a week later we came back through Eugene and accepted an invitation from her to participate in a workshop with her and Normandi Ellis. Normandi is a writer and literary scholar who has the ability to read and interpret hieroglyphs. She has the heart of a poet and a tremendous depth of understanding of the mysteries of Egypt and is the author of *Awakening Osiris, Feasts of Light, Dreams of Isis,* and other books. The Egyptian Mysteries workshop that Brad and I attended was titled "Becoming the Oracle"; it was designed to teach people how to open up and hone their skills as visionaries and oracular beings. In this "Becoming the Oracle" workshop, we were led on many shamanic journeys, which included the utilization of guided imagery and meditation.

I drop into altered states fairly easily, which I attribute not only to the natural abilities I've developed since childhood, but also to the Shamanic Breathwork sessions and altered-state journeys I have experienced over the years. On this particular guided journey, we were instructed to visualize the creator god Ptah as the source or wellspring from which the raw material of creation issues, and Isis as the organizing principle through which our reality is birthed in the constant rapture of creation. Using the metaphor of a wave to describe the universe and how our reality manifests, we were invited to dive deeply into that wave, where, with the assistance of the lioness goddess, Sekhmet, the feminine fire, we could entice extra raw material for the creation process from Ptah. Following this we could emerge from the wave into the presence of Isis and use our intention to experience any of the infinite vantage points available, including, with practice, positioning ourselves in front of the wave so that we could see what was coming.*

As I advanced to a position in front of the wave, I actually saw huge ocean breakers overcoming parts of the earth. Buildings were destroyed and many people and animals were drowning in what was an incredibly horrific vision. I felt that I was right there on an actual wave as it was crashing. At that time, little did I know that in December 2004 a tsunami would hit Thailand and that Nicki's stepson and his girlfriend would be caught up in it and perish, along with nearly a quarter million other people.

This was a very powerful meditative journey, and all the other participants came back from it seemingly just fine—except for me. I have undergone many, many spiritual journeys over the years, and "coming back" had not been a problem for quite some time. A couple of Nicki's alchemical healing practitioners and Normandi herself worked on me and really helped bring me back into my body, at which point I went outside and lay down on the earth, by a pond, to further ground me. At that time in my life, I wasn't focused on actively spending a lot of time seeing into the future to determine what was going to happen. However, I often had flashes of precognition in dreams and intuitive hits.

Sometimes in a Shamanic Breathwork session I will have a glimpse of what I call "previews of coming attractions." Oftentimes what I see is the immediate or near future. I'll have a sense that these visions are coming, but I am not *planning* to see them—they just occur.

Nicki has an ability to attract people to her who are, as she says, natural oracles. And while she doesn't credit herself as being primarily a visionary person in this way, she has an innate ability to guide others and be a catalyst for them to develop their oracular selves. She has done this with many of her students and other people she has worked with.

I saw Nicki as an alchemical spiritual midwife, and when she told me that I was one of the clearest oracular channels that she had ever

*For more detailed information on this guided meditation, see *Planetary Healing: Spirit Medicine for Global Transformation,* by Nicki Scully and Mark Hallert.

seen, she helped me to fully own that this was who I really was in my core essential self. I must admit that I had repressed this aspect of myself pretty deeply after my grandmother's death many years prior, but throughout the years this part of me had gradually reappeared, from time to time erupting and then going back underground until another episode would bring it up again. After my encounters with Nicki and our subsequent trip to Egypt in 2005, a few years later the oracle emerged fully, and I am happy to say, it has not gone into hiding again!

The process of doing this oracular work with Nicki gave me the opportunity to work through my fears that something bad might happen to me because of my prophetic gifts, or that I might cause something bad to happen. I was carrying leftover guilt ever since my Mammy died in the exact way and time that I had foreseen (as I discuss earlier in this book).

## ANSWERING AN ANCIENT CALL

My relationship with Nicki took a great turn and developed a lot further when Brad and I traveled to Egypt with her in 2005. There were many synchronicities that led to this seemingly sudden interest in Isis, Osiris, and their native land of Egypt. I, of course, had read about Isis, and through my studies, I knew that she was considered to be the greatest goddess of all time. Brad once had a Shamanic Breathwork experience wherein he had actually embodied and *become* Isis. This had allowed him to heal many of the past woundings that he had around women and his inner feminine, with one of the results being that he was very intrigued with Isis all of a sudden.

In 2003, Brad and I moved to North Carolina from California and bought property in a place called Iris Cove. Shortly after we moved in, we were at a little country gift store, and coincidentally we found a beautiful wooden hanging statue of Isis. We bought it and hung it at the entrance to our property, and then we changed the "r" in "Iris" to an "s"—and voila; we were now living at *Isis* Cove!

At that time I was working with my shamanic priestess colleague Anyaa

McAndrews, collaborating with her on a process called the Shamanic Priestess Process. In so doing, we were collectively working with a group of women who were in the process of becoming shamanic priestesses.

One day, quite spontaneously, Anyaa and I decided that we were going to take a group of priestesses to Egypt. I asked Nicki if she was available to organize and guide a trip for our circle. She was very excited about what I proposed, and very quickly our trip evolved from taking a group of priestesses to taking other friends too. We ended up with almost forty people, which is a considerable number to travel across Egypt for a couple of weeks!

Brad, Anyaa, and I looked at this as an opportunity to have a wonderful trip and the experience of a lifetime. We figured we would get to know Nicki better and benefit from going with her insofar as we would be able to learn from her wellspring of knowledge about the ancient mysteries. Nicki planned to take us to the most important sacred sites, many of which we would attend on private visits during off hours, so that we could delve into the mysteries in ritual, without the distraction of other tourists at the normally crowded monuments. We were also going to include some rituals of our own and bring in Shamanic Breathwork and the Shamanic Priestess Process.

That was our plan. Well . . . you know what they say about plans: "Make your plans and watch God laugh!"

## PARTING THE VEILS

Our flight path into Egypt took us over the Giza Plateau. I had a window seat and was looking down at the pyramids and the Sphinx as we descended, and all of a sudden I felt very spacey, very light-headed. I was dizzy and my vision was fuzzy. I thought I might be incredibly jet-lagged or that my blood sugar might be low.

We were due to arrive three days before most of the others in the group so that we could acclimate ourselves and get a feel for the place. When we got to our hotel, Nicki suggested that I pull the curtains and go to bed to rest, telling me that if I did that, no doubt I would feel better. And even though that's what I did, basically what happened was that, energetically, I was very altered.

In addition to having my energy zapped and moving in unpredictable ways throughout my body, I had problems with distorted vision and hearing. The only way I can describe it is that it was as if a gossamer veil was over my eyes, like I was looking through a smoky veiled atmosphere. And yet, as I was looking through it, I saw people, situations, and different things going on. At the same time, I was seeing energetic beings who, I eventually realized, were Egyptian archetypes fading in and out of my field of vision. It turns out that they were some of the most ancient shamanic gods of Egypt. I also saw the landscape differently. I saw it basically as it is today, but it also had some slight differences in aspect that made me realize that, at times, I was looking at an ancient version of the land.

It's not that I was seeing these things *instead* of what was there. I saw things that are there now and things that had been there at another time—one was overlaid on the top of the other. It was like putting one strip of film on top of another strip of film, distorting the image. This messed up my equilibrium and my depth perception, and it wreaked havoc with my hearing and all of my ordinary senses. In some ways it was reminiscent of the psychedelic trips I had taken in my younger years during the '60s and '70s.

But I was now in Egypt and I wasn't doing psychedelics.

I was the only person in our group to whom this was happening, and I was definitely in a very powerful altered state. I found it extremely difficult to breathe, and this made me feel very anxious. Although I was probably hyperventilating part of the time, there was definitely something else going on with my breathing that I couldn't explain. My chest and lungs were clear, but it was as if I was so out of my body that my body didn't know how to breathe.

Mohamed Nazmy is the wonderful owner and operator of Quest Travel, Nicki's partner and land agent in Egypt. He became so concerned about my condition that he brought his own doctor, a pulmonary specialist, to see me. This doctor advised that I might have to leave Egypt and return to the United States. When I heard this, an inner voice said to me, "This is a shamanic experience, and if you can hang in here and do this and *be* with this, you're going to have a rebirth. Something is here for you, and a healing is here for you. And you won't die, but if you leave Egypt, you *could* die." So I had to decide if I was going to listen to that inner voice or listen to my fear.

It wasn't easy, but I decided to listen to that inner voice. I stayed.

## THE SHAMANIC JOURNEY CONTINUES

Over the course of the next couple weeks, our group traveled throughout Egypt. We sailed for a number of days up the Nile River, visiting sacred sites and temples. Although we participated in some of the rituals we had planned, our itinerary changed drastically from our original intentions.

The main reason it changed is because one evening, probably the second evening we were there, Nicki and everyone else began to realize that my condition was very serious, that I was not getting any better, and that traditional medicine did not seem to help my strange illness. The majority of the people in our group had come to Egypt to do Shamanic Breathwork with me, and yet most days I didn't even have the strength to get out of bed—let alone teach breathwork! Time was running out; soon the rest of our group would arrive, and our tour would officially begin.

We were trying to figure out what to do when I revealed to Nicki that I had had a compelling, intense dream that may have foretold what was happening to me. In the dream I met a tall, muscular being with canine features, which I interpreted at the time as being part man and part wolf. He was a very powerful, wise being who was also very darkskinned and beautiful. He wasn't malevolent at all, and didn't scare me; however, he had very obviously shown up to give me a message and take me through some kind of shamanic experience.

This being came to me and told me that my heart needed to be renewed because it was too heavy with the burdens of the past experiences of my life. He then told me that he was going to heal it and proceeded to take a sharp stone and cut it out—which didn't hurt me physically at all in the dream. He then gave my heart to a dark feminine figure, his birth mother, who put it into some sort of jar. Later on I came to know that this was a traditional canopic jar.

Nicki was fascinated by my dream. She knew immediately that it was Anubis who had come to me. She went on to tell me that on the plane, she had been reading about ancient shamanic ceremonies that had taken place in Sakkara and other places in Egypt. They reminded her of my dream. What struck her in particular was that some of the very specific visions I was having sounded very similar to what she had been reading about in the book. And yet there was no way I had any prior knowledge of the information she was reading. Being one who values the path of direct experience, I seldom read about a place before I go to it, which allows me to look at it with fresh eyes and an open mind and heart.

Nicki was excited about what she was reading, and rather unexpectedly an amazing synchronicity occurred, which resulted in her being granted a special permit to allow our group into Egypt's most ancient pyramid—the step pyramid at Sakkara!

Brad and Anyaa were taking good care of me, given my altered state, and were never very far from my side. Meanwhile, Nicki realized that something extraordinary was afoot, and through me, she called upon her teacher, Thoth, the Egyptian god of wisdom, language, and communications. Thoth had been the architect behind Nicki's teachings on both alchemical healing and her work with the Egyptian Mysteries for more than two decades.* "What does Thoth have to say about what is going on?" she asked me.

---

*For more on Nicki Scully's teachings, please see *Alchemical Healing: A Guide to Spiritual, Physical, and Transformational Medicine*.

## THOTH SPEAKS

Immediately, without missing a beat, even though I really didn't have much of an idea who Thoth was, I started talking, but I was having difficulty breathing as I spoke. I was gasping and coughing, and I felt very weak. After a few minutes of allowing Thoth to speak, I began to relax very deeply and felt as if I was lifting up out of my body.

The next thing I knew, Nicki told me that two hours had gone by, and I had been talking the entire time. At the outset, she had picked up her laptop and started typing everything I said. (Nicki had been scribing the visions of her husband and many other seers for decades, so she could type very quickly, even with her eyes closed.)

Everything that Thoth said through me, Nicki typed. Anubis had begun to chime in too; he outlined the details of a ceremony that he wanted us to perform at Sakkara—a re-enactment of Anubis's ritual from my dream. This was a very important ritual initiation that was to be given to our group.

According to Anubis, Thoth and Nephthys (Anubis's mother) were to participate in this ritual as well. The idea was to work with those who wished to undergo alchemical transformation so that they might receive greater wisdom and a direct connection with divinity, which would lead to immortality. Isis then had the sacred task of carefully transporting the canopic jar—which held the initiate's heavy or wounded heart—to the temple on Elephantine Island in Aswan in the south of Egypt and present it to the great ram-headed craftsman and master potter Khnum, the Egyptian deity to whom that temple is dedicated.

In this ceremony, which members of our group would participate in, Khnum was to skillfully craft a new physical body and infuse it with ka.* Part of the renewal would be created by expanding the awareness of the initiate to see their bigger story and give meaning to everything that had happened to them thus far in their lives.

---

*The ka body is the life-force energy of an individual, which comes into being at a person's birth. In ancient Egypt, it was often depicted as a twin.

Creating a new body for each individual initiate and infusing that vessel with ka was the first step in preparing the person to later receive his or her regenerated heart.* It would take several days before the initiates would be ready to receive their renewed hearts, during which time other rites and initiations would be performed by them. Many of these rituals were derived directly from my visions, while others were adapted from Nicki's vast repertoire of Egyptian mystery rites.

Some people maintain that the reenactment of a very significant ritual such as this one from my dream serves as a metaphor; however, others have speculated about the longevity of some of the pharaohs. This speculation leads me to believe that a veil of mystery surrounds the actual physical death of the pharaoh, as well as the metaphorical death and rebirth rituals, as they attempted to "make the word flesh," in other words, to create the immortal embodied spirit—on Earth as it is in Heaven.

It was Nicki's belief that this specific ceremony had never actually happened, although she also believed that it may have been downloaded to me in order to speed up the transformation of individual consciousness in much the same way as was done for the pharaohs in the ancient Heb Sed festivals.

Nicki also felt very strongly that this circumstance of my altered reality was directly related to the Old Kingdom rites of renewal. This would mandate that our trip would be radically different from others that had come before; it would prove to grant us a unique itinerary that would become the basis for two books that she and I would go on to write together.

That first night that Thoth and Anubis spoke through me, Nicki said to me, "I think we should enact the ceremonies that you are describing so that the participants will understand and be better prepared for the initiation they will receive."

So we cast ourselves in a sort of Shamanic Ceremonial Theater. Nicki is deeply connected to the lineage of Thoth and was happy to allow his energies to flow through her. Each of us played different archetypes,

---

*For specific information on these later rituals, please see *Shamanic Mysteries of Egypt*, by Nicki Scully and Linda Star Wolf.

depending on the ritual. One time I was the initiate ready to surrender my old, outworn heart to be renewed. Another time I was Queen Holy Mother Isis and the mighty golden lioness Sekhmet. Brad often stepped in as Anubis, and Anyaa frequently identified with the mysterious Nephthys, although at different times they became different personas.

The four of us were a shamanic team, and the collective journey we agreed to undertake was one of faith, because none of us was certain that I'd even be well enough to show up at the temple to perform the ritual that had been downloaded the day before. We all took it one day at a time.

After each ceremony that we eventually undertook, which also served as a downloading session, I was in such an altered state that it was difficult for me to return to normal consciousness. It took more than a few minutes of Brad and others I was close to on the trip squeezing my hands and feet before I was able to come back to myself. Brad often became very concerned because during these experiences I got very cold and, at times, could barely breathe.

He felt triggered in that he was having a past-life recall wherein the two of us were performing some form of research in ancient Egypt that involved the exploration of immortality, and something went very wrong. I actually died during an experiment or ritual. In the beginning, whenever I went into the altered state to commune with and channel Thoth, Brad would start nodding out and would appear to be deeply asleep throughout most of the downloading. We were so connected energetically that he simply couldn't stay awake. It was upsetting for him, and he was scared for my well-being. I think he was dissociating, or vicariously he was so closely connected to me that he was going *with* me, somehow, to the other side.

## CEREMONY TO RENEW THE HEART
## AT SAKKARA

As scheduled, the rest of the group arrived on the third day I was in Egypt. The plan was to all have dinner together and pass around a talking stick so that everyone could get acquainted with one another. I somehow managed to get through that dinner and co-lead the group meditation, which included drumming and the talking stick circle.

As soon as the circle was over, I had to return to my room, and once again Nicki, Brad, Anyaa, and I gathered to see what new information was ready to unfold. I lay in a semitrance state upon my bed in the Mena House Oberoi Hotel, within sight of the pyramids and the Sphinx on the Giza Plateau.

The following morning, according to our plan, we took our group to the Sphinx and held a powerful opening ritual ceremony where we paid our respects to the great guardian. I remember feeling fine up until the time that we finished the ritual, at which point our wonderful Egyptologist, Emil, did his part by sharing his knowledge with our group. It was then I realized that I was in a highly altered state and could not take in a word he said. Once again my depth perception was way off, making it hard to walk or to stand up for very long. In addition, my breathing felt incredibly shallow.

The following day we were due to go to Sakkara for our first major initiation ceremony to begin the renewal of the heart (which I talk about earlier in this chapter).

As we entered the sacred site before sunset, I had a deep feeling of déjà vu and an inner sensation that somehow we had been here and done this ceremony before. I felt that we were probably symbolically reenacting the shamanic mystery of the removal and renewal of the heart that may have been done on this same spot thousands of years past.

When we arrived at Sakkara, I lay down on a slab of concrete outside of the pyramid. I was dressed in a white gown for my archetypal role, which was that of the innocent dove, the trusting one who comes to meet Anubis. As of this writing, entry into the step pyramid has not yet become open to the public, and when we were there in 2005, only a few highly privileged VIPs and scholars had been allowed into the ancient, rough-hewn bowels of the structure, which is almost five thousand years old. Our plan was to have a walk-through of the ritual so everyone would know what to expect of the actual ceremony that would subsequently take place inside the pyramid itself.

When we set up to perform our reenactment outside, the guards who protect these sites were watching us from a distance. They continued to watch the transformations as Brad became Anubis, the surgeon who cut out the heart of the initiate and gave it to Anyaa, the high priestess Nephthys, who worked her magic on the heart before carefully placing it in the canopic jar. Nicki as Thoth narrated the rite, directing and articulating the instructions describing the events as they were occurring in the sacred ceremony.

When this was over, we all proceeded into the ancient, crumbling pyramid and made our way down the narrow hallway into its belly. Once inside, we did some Shamanic Breathwork and guided journeying, with everyone lying on the floor. At this time, everyone in attendance was invited to surrender their old heart to Anubis and be anointed as they underwent the beginning ritual of the renewal of the heart.

After we drummed, played music, and created a sacred space, Brad, as Anubis, performed the surgery and symbolically removed each participant's heart. This was at the beginning of our trip, and other than a few members of the group who I already had a close relationship with, no one knew what I personally was going through in terms of my highly altered state. Neither did they know that a good portion of what we were doing had not been done before on these trips.

While Nicki had certainly done scores of ceremonies at the sacred sites and temples, she'd never done this specific extended ritual in this exact way. I truly honor her courage, insight, and ability to trust the process in leading these ceremonies at each monument as we made the journey together into the other worlds.

The ceremony inside the Sakkara pyramid lasted at least an hour, and in total, we were there for several hours. During the entire time I was able to be present and be in ceremonial space just fine; however, as soon as we broke, I could barely stand upright. Never knowing how I was going to feel added a whole other layer of stress. In addition, when I participated in each initiation, I most often felt as if I actually *was* the particular deity I was representing. I believe this was due to my openness and vulnerability and how easily I would drop into a zone wherein the energies of the respective deity were channeled through me.

Everyone else may have been acting, but I wasn't. And I didn't see the others for who they were—I responded to the archetype they were playing. In addition, the rites that I participated in didn't resemble anything I'd seen in any book about ancient Egypt. Instead, I could see *through* them at some level; I perceived the entire ceremony through a prism of the past.

That was my experience throughout the trip. I can say that I rallied at times, and when I say "rallied," I mean it felt like I was getting a bit better—perhaps I was breathing better—or I felt more hopeful that I *might* be getting better. Some days I had more energy than others, like the day we went to the Cairo Museum. And a few times when we went out to eat I might have some strength for a while. But it wouldn't last long, and every night, when I began to download the esoteric material with Nicki, I felt very stressed out. However, the only way to gain relief was to let the messages come through.

Even though antibiotics have always been problematic for me, my Egyptian physician insisted that I take them. He believed I might have an infection, although beyond that he was unable to figure out what was going on. I was desperate enough to try them, hoping that they might help, but they proved ineffectual. Several of the women in our group were Reiki practitioners, and they performed Reiki on me in the evenings. While that helped some, ultimately I just had to let go and trust the process.

At that time, I think that Nicki, more than anyone else, understood what was happening to me. She has such a strong connection to both the shamanic world and to Egypt, and it felt like our shamanic souls were bonding in a sacred purpose. I, however, felt very embarrassed because I had been instrumental in bringing many of the people in this group to Egypt, with the promise of teaching them how to do Shamanic Breathwork, with the added benefit of doing those breathing exercises in the sacred temples of this great land. Now something was wrong with my own breathing, and I couldn't even really breathe normally, let alone practice breathwork!

It was pretty ironic, and I felt like I had been hit below the belt. When I thought about it more, I realized that the archetypal energies I was channeling had gone right to my Achilles heel in order to get my attention and give me the experience I was most afraid of: not being able to breathe! In hindsight it all made perfect sense, for it became the perfect shamanic initiation, one that I had called into my field of experience as I sought to renew my own heart.

## THE ULTIMATE TRIP OF ALCHEMICAL TRANSFORMATION

The remainder of our time in Egypt was spent leading our group on a wide variety of experiences, which included Shamanic Breathwork, various initiation ceremonies, guided journeys, and other rites of passage. Our pilgrimage culminated with a very special initiation during a private, after-hours ritual in the Great Pyramid. There, in the King's Chamber, held within the walls of what is perhaps the most powerful building on the planet, we underwent a journey of alchemical transformation: the transmutation and illumination of ourselves as pharaoh.*

Once inside the pyramid, we climbed to the King's Chamber, where each member of the group took turns lying in the sarcophagus, and in so doing, we expressed our willingness to continue to die to everything that

---

*For more information, please see *Shamanic Mysteries of Egypt,* by Nicki Scully and Linda Star Wolf.

had come before, to everything we had ever known. In the beginning of our journey, we surrendered our hearts and spent much of our time releasing inner conflicts and preparing to receive illumination. This was done in order to be resurrected and go back out into the world with our now enlightened hearts fully activated and intact.

This was the final opportunity on this tour to completely surrender our old selves and open to the imaginal cells. In this, we not only had the intention of becoming wisdom keepers, embracing pharaonic divine energy, but of bringing the heart/mind of God into whatever situation was before us. In some ways you could say we were able to willingly turn to our higher power's divine will and become empowered to live in the world with an inner authority guiding our daily actions and decisions.

This ceremony in the Great Pyramid was very intense, and when it was over I began to feel a little better. We left Egypt a few days later and arrived back in the United States in time to celebrate Thanksgiving. Once back in North Carolina I slowly began to come back into myself, and then, in late January, I started having the same strange symptoms again. In February I received another dream and an inner message from the Egyptian archetypes: I heard clearly that I was supposed to write a book that would share the ancient renewal rituals of the heart. I was told that the archetypes were preparing to come forward to help all those who were ready to renew their hearts and open to higher frequencies to help usher in the changing of the ages that was upon us.

I contacted Nicki and shared this information with her. Shortly thereafter we commenced work on a book together, drawing upon the material that I had downloaded during our time together in Egypt as well as information that I would continue to download. In this, I surrendered again to the process, like the archetype of the Dove, the Initiate, so that I could receive channeled information about the ancient rituals and shapeshift into the Enlightened Heart Shaman Anubis, who walks between the worlds. Nicki, for her part, held the space of Thoth, the sacred scribe.

The material that this generated was to form our first book on this topic, *Shamanic Mysteries of Egypt*. In the book we featured many deities and discussed them in the order that they had been introduced to us. Each offered a specific rite that, all together, prepared us to become divine, illumined, fully realized humans. Then we added the eight major initiations and addressed how one could use all of this material in an oracular fashion.

Because Nicki was on the West Coast and I was on the East Coast, we came up with a daily schedule wherein we would work over the phone long distance. I would call Nicki and then lean back in my chair or lie down, and we would breathe the heart breath that is used as the invocation for each rite in the book to return to an altered state similar to the one I had been in during our time in Egypt. Nicki and I would discuss my download of the additional information as she scribed it, put it in context according to her experience and knowledge, and shape it into a book.

Working in this way, we finished *Shamanic Mysteries of Egypt* in a few short months in 2006. When I step back and examine the entirety of all that happened and the very real suffering I experienced, I have to look at the sacred purpose behind it. I believe that the shamanic initiation and portal that I experienced took place so that I could open up more fully and share my visions and the powerful heart rituals to renew the heart chakra of humanity.

And I believe that's exactly what happened. Not only did Nicki and I write *Shamanic Mysteries of Egypt,* we ended up writing another book together titled *The Anubis Oracle,* which includes thirty-five cards illustrated by Kris Waldherr, who was able to capture my visions with remarkable skill and accuracy. And later, with my friend and respected colleague Ruby Falconer, I wrote *Shamanic Egyptian Astrology.* Ruby has more than thirty years as a master astrologer under her belt, and her expertise in this area broke new ground as we recast ancient astrological practices in the new light of the shamanic mysteries of the ancient Egyptians.

I also like to think that I underwent this extraordinary journey because the archetypes and deities are our ancient ancestors who love us and are here to help us through the turning of the ages, this critical time in our planet's history. In my case, and as stated previously but bears repeating, they wanted to heal my deepest wounds relating to death and to my gift of being an oracle. They also wanted to rid me, once and for all, of the belief that, because my grandmother had died in the place and manner I had envisioned in my nighttime dream, that I had caused her death.

They wanted this information to come through, and not necessarily from an academic standpoint—although Nicki certainly knows her stuff when it comes to the legends, myths, and deities of Egypt. The message that kept coming to me was that they wanted our books to come through, from an *inner experience,* to demonstrate how everyone, everywhere can learn the powerful principles and sacred inner wisdom associated with the ancient Egyptian mystery schools. In other words, we all have an inner Egypt, where we can connect directly to the same source that is drawn upon in the ancient healing rituals and ceremonies. I also don't think we were supposed to focus solely on the shamanic Egyptian rituals.

## AKASHIC ACCESS AND IMMORTALITY

The deities repeatedly communicated that we all have an inner healer and an inner visionary shaman wisdom keeper that's in touch with the Akashic Records, who can download this information freely whenever it's needed. We all can train ourselves to do this, to have access to the imaginal cells in order to pull our future to us in a more realized and accelerated way, using modalities like Shamanic Breathwork and the nonlocal mind.

I also believe that in ancient Egypt there were yogis and yoginis, adepts who could come and go through different dimensions very easily. They could move from the present to the past or future and back again.

I believe this was happening during the Old Kingdom in Egypt, but something went awry, and things didn't quite work out the way they had been envisioned.

From my own inner revelations and from what Nicki has said, these yogis and yoginis worked with the pharaohs, helping to renew them and to keep them connected to divinity, perhaps indefinitely. The material that I channeled informed me that, over time, this process spread to include the very wealthy, the elite of ancient Egypt, and then began to be performed on society at large.

If you study esoteric traditions the world over, you come to see parallels in that groups of people, throughout the written annals of history, desired immortality. Many are on record as having lived very long lives, such as Enoch, who is mentioned in Genesis 5:21–24: "When Enoch had lived 65 years, he fathered Methuselah. Enoch walked with God after he fathered Methuselah 300 years and had other sons and daughters. Thus all the days of Enoch were 365 years."

Jesus also talked about achieving immortal life, leading one to wonder about his context for this discussion. Some texts claim that Jesus spent many years in Egypt studying the mystery teachings there. A concept such as "on Earth as it is in Heaven" seems particularly relevant in that it seems to suggest that attempts were being made to bring the invisible world to the visible world and to teach about immortality: at some point people would cease to die and Heaven would come to Earth.

Thus it seems to me that the cults of old were in part working to create immortality. That's why there was such a fascination with the dead and the sarcophagi and mummies. However, my inner sense is that this line of exploration derailed somewhere along the way. Things went wrong due to an abuse of power, and the entire endeavor backfired and collapsed.

I believe this happened in Atlantis; it may have happened in Lemuria; and it happened in Egypt and the Americas too. Great cities, whether Mayan, Aztec, or Egyptian, were seemingly suddenly abandoned. Some scholars attribute this to natural phenomena, such as comets hitting the earth, climate change, or great floods. This may well be so, but I also believe that, in conjunction with these natural disasters, humankind may have abused its power in experiments with immortality. Perhaps this corruption in some way *caused* the natural disasters.

Of course, other scholars, seers, and visionaries have bandied some of this about. However, I don't believe that anyone has put forth the premise that catastrophic events happened *because* humankind derailed in its attempts to become immortal like the gods, or in its attempts to achieve a state where one could move from past to present to future at will.

As we evolve, we don't move in a circle and we don't move in a straight line—we move in a pattern of spiral dynamics. And I believe that today we're at a similar point on the wheel: we are poised on the brink of a collective decision, however unconscious it may be. We are at the point Atlantis was just before it sank and the point where the ancient Egyptians were when they began to lose their direct connection with their pantheon, their ancestral principles. We're at that same point in that we have a lot of advanced technology, we've evolved to a certain level, and we're either going to make the wise decisions that weren't made at those prior times in Atlantis and ancient Egypt or we're going to sink again.

With regard to this, Nicki asked me, "What could make the difference? How could we *not* go down that same path again?" I received the following message very clearly: "We must learn to think with our hearts." Nicki replied, "Ah, yes, that would be Ptah"—the one who creates from his heart.

# 9

# THE DUAT

## *On Earth as It Is in Heaven*

*I*n one of my deep shamanic journeys, a profound understanding of the duat came to me in a very powerful way: In the moment that everything is born in this world, it has a corollary in the mind and heart of God. It has a psychic blueprint with a very high frequency. Grandmother Twylah called the place from which it arose the Field of Plenty. That which is seeking to be born on Earth must travel through the energies of water, earth, fire, and air to come into a density of matter and an earthly form. It then becomes activated by spirit and is alive here on the earth plane.

Some teach that the Duat refers to the manifest world we live in, coupled with an underworld composed of bad experiences or difficult trials and tribulations. My own inner mystical journeys informed me that the Duat does consist of two worlds, but they are much more alike than different. The Duat consists primarily of the original blueprint of that which is born, and then the thing itself, which manifests here on Earth.

Scholars Robert Bauval and Adrian Gilbert, in their book *The Orion Mystery,* propose that the Giza pyramids were built in a pattern that mimics the stars in the constellation Orion. This is a perfect *symbolic* example of my interpretation of the Duat: as above, so below. To the ancient Egyptians, there was no division; it was just their world. Their *unified* world. Earth was a reflection of the heavenly world. We've got eternity to be in oneness with the Godhead, but the human experience—where spirit is *in form*—is, and was considered to be, a sacred experience.

Our task as human beings is to manifest the Duat. So when we say, "Our Father who art in Heaven, hallowed be thy name; thy kingdom come; thy will be done, on Earth as it is in Heaven," we're asking for God's will, and we're asking for the manifestation of the original blueprint of what exists in the infinite spiritual world of God's mind. On Earth when we say, "Make Thy will my will" we are asking for help by invoking our guides to turn the ego agendas we have formed in our lives over to our soul's original imprint.

Our task as human beings is to manifest the Duat as above, so below; as within, so without. When you bring together the above, the below, the within, and the without, you're gathering the four directions. In bringing the duality of above and below together with the duality of within and without, a sacred union is formed through the unified field it creates.

## THE SECRET OF THE TRINITY

If you bring two opposites together, you produce the divine third, something bigger than the two opposites you started with. For instance, if two people have a disagreement, they each bring a point of view to the table. In discussing their differences, they may arrive at a compromise: a new third thing. When we humans merge our dual nature, our opposites, we create what Carl Jung referred to as a sacred marriage within, and in so doing we produce the third thing, which is a higher level of consciousness.

This is the secret of the trinity and the spiral path of shamanic psychospiritual transformation: the three in one. But it's the principle of the Duat, of the two, that makes the one into the three and the three into the one over and over again. This is a very important concept to understand because it is a fundamental and dynamic principle of our shamanic universe. Carl Jung expressed his thoughts about the core of the universe being dual in its essential nature and proposed that this duality is sacred as well as profane.

However, most people focus on oneness and do not want to do the difficult work to discover how duality, with its often extreme tension of opposites, forces a sacred union and reconciliation within our psyches and our hearts.

Both the sacred and the profane aspects of the Duat are part of our journey. The great mythologist and author Joseph Campbell would say that it's the hero's journey, a path that contains both the light and the dark; through meeting its challenges, true wisdom may be attained.

Another key point is that in order for spirit to have a human experience, there *must* be duality. Creator spirit didn't create anything by accident. That's why there can't be original sin as it's been taught in some fundamentalist religions. There is no original sin, or if there is, it has been grossly misunderstood. Mathew Fox, the internationally acclaimed theologian and author, says that we are born in "original blessing."

Some might consider all I've said about duality to be heretical because it implies that God is not always perfect and that God desires to grow. Well, think about it for a minute. If we are created in God's image, we are going to grow up someday to be *like* God, and we are going to have experiences so that we can grow spiritually, don't you think we might have the characteristics of the mother and father who made us? And don't you think that one of the main characteristics of our mother and our father (God) is to grow—beyond God's original impulse?

God wanted to have experiences, not just sit there in eternal oneness. It wanted to be even more than what it already was. So even God, if you will, likes to dance the dance of life. In the Hindu religion there is a term that describes this state. *Leela* is the divine play of cosmic consciousness living out life *in form*.

In an earlier chapter, I referenced the account of Mellen-Thomas Benedict, a man who died for an hour and a half and received spiritual insights during the time he was technically dead. I draw upon his further revelations here, because he too was shown that we are all God reinventing God:

> Creation is God exploring God's Self through every way imaginable, in an ongoing, infinite exploration through every one of us. I began to see during my near-death experience that everything that is, is the Self, literally, your Self, my Self. Everything is the great Self. That is why God knows even when a leaf falls. That is possible because wherever you are is the center of the universe. Wherever any atom is, that is the center of the universe. There is God in that. . . . We are literally God exploring God's self in an infinite Dance of Life. Your uniqueness enhances all of Life.*

The minute God split off from itself, duality was born. And the minute that happened, there was God and there was the other. But I believe that God knew that the other was also God.

I'm using the word *God*, but we can call God the Great Mystery, the One Source, or whatever feels sacred. After it had created "the other" (part of itself), that other then split off into four energies: earth, air, fire, and water, because it immediately knew what it needed to do in order to create matter and inform the spiraling universe.

## THE INFINITY OF CONSCIOUSNESS

There is no limit to how far God's consciousness can expand. And in *our* human experiences, there's no limit to how far we can go in consciousness as long as we're connecting with the mind and heart of God. This experience of spiritual expansion happens through duality, through the constant build up, tension, and resolution of opposites. The experience of spiritual expansion doesn't happen in oneness. Think about it. When you are in oneness, you are much more inclined to sit around

---

*Please see www.mellen-thomas.com for more information.

and meditate and feel good about where you are. There's no need to change. We're not restless; we're not bored; we're happy with no conflict. Oneness is a fantastic experience.

For a time.

But then we *might* get a little bored; we *might* get a bit restless. We get tired of meditating and want to try something different. And wanting to do something different is a natural urge toward further growth. In our growing, we will come up against resistance, something that creates tension. Then we will have to find our way through this part of the journey. So the journey of the human being to become more Godlike—at least on this planet so far—is activated through the tension of opposites. But you can't just hold the tension: you must reconcile it. And when you reconcile it, you see that you're just dealing with two sides of the same coin, over and over again.

Every time you see that, you merge into oneness again—the divine third—because you've produced a higher level of consciousness for yourself. Your old consciousness is just lying there dead on the floor. You become a new being. People speak of becoming a new being in Christ or developing the Buddha mind. Every time this happens you go into the oneness—the whole divine oneness of remembering who you really are.

But there's more. I believe that every time every being on this planet—and in any other dimension—has a sacred marriage, the energy of that funnels back to the Godhead, and that's how God grows *through* us. Because we're its sacred ideas who are remembering our blueprint, we're God's experience on Earth. We mysteriously replenish God's energy through our own evolution. The reason some people would deem that heretical is because, according to their view, we're born in sin. That we could actually *feed God* is blasphemy to them. Well, of course we're feeding God! That's what the infinity symbol (also known as the lemniscate) represents: our human experience is feeding God, and God's divine experience is simultaneously feeding us.

We're God's children, but when we remember who we are, we're also God incarnated as the Christed energy itself: God's thoughts. We belong to God—there is no separation. I like to imagine God is enjoying the experience immensely. This source of all creation understands that a certain amount of forgetfulness, spiritual amnesia, and suffering must be gone through in order to experience the joy. And isn't that what *we* learn? If we do hard work and do what we need to do, then we have victory? Victory would not be very victorious without at least a *little* struggle. And that butterfly could never fly without some struggling to work its way out of its cocoon, which helped to pump the fluid into its newly emerging wings.

With duality, the tensions can get very strong—and we know how *that* feels. We get very emotional; we get very intense—we even create wars out of this energy. We need to understand that this is an alchemical process that is mainly happening inside of us, but fate will step up to show us that we are projecting these qualities out onto the world around us; we're all creating this cosmic *Leela* play together. We're gods ourselves, and our thoughts are blueprints. The more quickly we realize this, the more quickly we will evolve by taking responsibility for our consciousness and functioning as co-creators with God, instead of being codependent bystanders. Instead of not having power, we *own* our power.

When we are codependent we give away our power by focusing on other people or situations, not ourselves. We look to other people or other situations as being the problem: The president is the problem; the oil company is the problem; the terrorists are the problem. Instead, we need to acknowledge that these entities have become the outer figureheads of our inner consciousness.

Then we might say to ourselves, "What do I want to do about this?" Knowing that if we look inside we will learn how we can effect change, we now decide to create a different reality. By accessing the Duat through the imaginal world, we will be able to see the original blueprint so that we can be the architect of that new reality here on Earth.

We can look in a mirror and see ourselves, but we can never see ourselves the way others do. Perhaps, without us, God can't see itself either; we are God's true mirror. The Duat is a very important concept to understand in that there is already a future self, of each of us, in the mind and heart of God, and that future self was created when God split apart from itself. In this way our future is also our very distant past.

This sacred blueprint is already contained within the mind and heart of God, and that's the mystery that we live through each and every day. It's our task to clear the obstacles from our true understanding of this, because when we do, our outer reality will match our inner experience, and Heaven indeed will be right here on Earth.

# 10

# THE SACRED GEOMETRY OF SHAMANIC PSYCHOSPIRITUAL TRANSFORMATION

As I said earlier in the book, I believe that all human beings possess a shamanic spirit. All of us have the ability to walk between the worlds and to develop our humanity and our spirituality at the same time. However, whatever we do, whether it's sitting behind a desk and pushing paper, becoming an activist, baking bread, or meditating all day, if the heart's not involved, then we're not fully present and we're not fully alive the way I believe we were intended to be.

The heart is the secret gateway between the worlds and determines how open or closed we are in our approach to life. The heart has to open to allow us to travel between different levels of consciousness. Often when people are dedicated to meditation they reach very high levels of spiritual consciousness. They can become so expanded that they may not realize they still have a human body or basic human needs. This may be the path of some people in that they are called to work in their upper chakras. Conversely, it may be other people's path to be totally oriented in the other direction: to the three lower chakras. These people may be so hedonistic that they become completely consumed by their addictions and fall into abuse of not only themselves but also the earth's resources and other beings.

What does all this have to do with learning from the future and drawing our future to us? Well, if we're not able to navigate between the worlds, between the upper and lower chakras, then we're going to be trapped in one world of being or the other. We're going to have lofty high ideals, we might even be able to envision the future, but we won't have any roots. We won't have a way to communicate with the lower chakras, which are supposed to carry out the mandate of the higher ones.

I was introduced to the six-pointed star many years ago by my first breathwork teacher, Jacquelyn Small. I well remember the rush of energy that flowed through my chakras while I listened to her explain how when all the chakras work in harmony with one another (which is symbolized by the six-pointed star, as we will see below) they have the power to transform our lives in amazing ways. This geometric symbol has appeared at pivotal times of huge transformation for me, so I know it is a very portent archetypal soul symbol for my personal journey.

## THE ALCHEMY OF THE CHAKRAS

Let's take a closer look at the chakras and the sacred geometry of shamanic psychospiritual transformation. First we will examine the lower three chakras: the root chakra; the lower abdomen, or sacral, chakra; and the solar plexus.

The first chakra, known as the root chakra, is the focal point of our survival and our safety. It connects us to the earth, and when it is in balance, we feel grounded. The root chakra also helps us manifest our purpose on Earth. The second chakra is the sacral chakra, concerned with our sexuality and our sense of self. It's also the focal point for how we relate to others, our emotions, and our creativity. The third chakra is the solar plexus chakra. It is where we hold our personal power and where our ego resides, as well as our passions and impulses, our anger and our strengths.

I envision these three lower chakras as an upside down triangle with the top of the tip pointing toward the earth.

The top three chakras, on the other hand, make up a second triangle, right side up with the tip pointing heavenward; it comprises the fifth, sixth, and seventh chakras. The fifth chakra is the throat, or etheric, chakra and is related to communication and an authentic expression of oneself; when it is blocked we are not able to fully express needs and desires. The sixth chakra is known as the third eye, or brow, chakra, and as such it is related to physical sight as well as intuitive insight, to things that we know without really understanding how we know them. It is often referred to as the celestial chakra. The seventh chakra is the crown chakra, or ketheric chakra, which provides our connection to the larger world beyond our body. It is said that our soul enters our body through the crown chakra at birth and leaves through it when we die.

When the two triangles converge and integrate into one harmonious system, a six-pointed star is created. The six-pointed star has long been a powerful symbol for many religious and spiritual traditions in various cultures the world over.

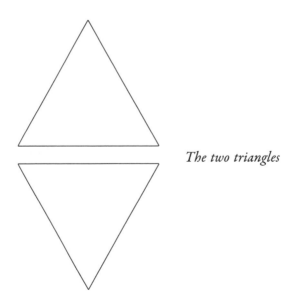

*The two triangles*

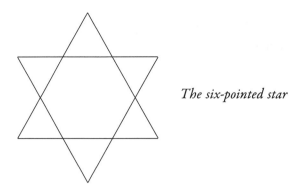

*The six-pointed star*

For shamanic psychospiritual integration between our upper and lower chakras to occur, the bottom triangle must move upward and the upper triangle downward. In so doing, however, the top of the upper triangle point remains above the rest of the star, pointing heavenward, and the lower triangle point remains outside of the rest of the star, pointing down toward the earth. This is very meaningful symbolically in that it demonstrates that the lower chakras, our very human part, don't lose themselves completely in the spiritual realms, and our upper chakras, which are typically connected to the more spiritual expression of our being, don't become lost in the human part of who we are.

These two very different aspects of ourselves must connect and communicate with one another, get to know and accept one another, and even come to love one another. However, they are separate for a reason, meaning that they each have a special function in the evolution of consciousness and do not need to be totally absorbed into each other.

If you rotate the six-pointed star around like a wheel, you will see it is true in every direction. You don't lose being human or spiritual, but you begin an integration and a communication between the two polarities of each line.

What makes this integration and communication possible is the fourth chakra, in the middle, which is the heart. The fourth chakra is the center of love, spirituality, and compassion. As such, it determines our ability to love others as well as ourselves.

When we're feeling lost and don't know which steps to take next in our lives, these triangles can feel really far apart. The reality is that we feel this way because there is a disconnect between our upper chakras and our lower chakras. If we are trying to make a decision, and the decision is not filtered through the heart, we either identify with our upper chakras in making the decision, or we identify with our lower chakras.

The lower chakras are all about our wants and needs on a very basic level. If I identify with my lower chakras, I can be brutish and nasty and aggressive and uncaring and run roughshod over things, or I can just be stuck in the muck and be anxious or depressed or feeling like a victim, or greedy and power-hungry and out for myself. Many addictions are based in the realm of the lower chakras, as well as acting out and sex abuse, and all kinds of power plays.

The attitude for those who relate mainly to the lower chakras is often that of "We're just human beings; there's no such thing as God; it's all science; when you die, you rot, and that's it." This is a breeding ground for apathy.

Alternatively, one can become polarized in the light of the upper three chakras. Sometimes it's very hard for people to wrap their minds around how that could be bad, or wrong, or dysfunctional. This is called being in spiritual bypass. People in spiritual bypass forget that they have a human side; they pursue spirituality to an extreme degree and think that they're supposed to become the Dalai Lama. They feel they are always supposed to be kind and nice.

These people have an attitude that can be summed up as follows: "We're not really human; we're just spirit, and that's all we are." They'll say, "This human experience is simply not that important, and we just need to be really good and go to church on Sunday. The rapture is coming, and animals are just animals, and trees are nice, but it's okay to cut them down because they're not spiritual; only human beings are spiritual."

Well, this is an abdication of their responsibility and a denial of their humanity.

We can make spirituality an intellectual pursuit; many Buddhists become very devoted and meditate for hours at a time. However, it's worth noting that many people who spend that much time in the upper realms become so detached and dissociated that they have difficulty relating to the world around them in a truly warm, compassionate, and heartfelt manner. They live in their heads, and they're not in touch with the reality of this world at all. I really have a reaction to the philosophy that maintains "It's all an illusion; none of it really matters. It's all part of the great karmic wheel of transformation." Well, yes. But we're *here,* and perhaps part of our reason for being here is that we're supposed to be involved in *this* world. And how do we know that? Maybe because we're here!

## THE SACRED ROLE OF THE VISIONARY

Angeles Arrien is an anthropologist, educator, and author. She also acts as a consultant to many groups and institutions. Her work centers on teaching about four main archetypes: the Warrior, the Teacher, the Healer, and the Visionary. In her work she discusses the attributes of each archetype. Her teachings direct us to "show up, pay attention, speak the truth, and stay open to the outcome."

For the purposes of this discussion, I would like to emphasize the archetype she has identified as the Visionary and the important role of the Visionary in our world.

> The task of the visionary is to tell the truth without blame or judgment. Truthfulness, authenticity, and integrity are essential keys to developing our vision and intuition. We express the Way of the Visionary through personal creativity, goals, plans, and our ability to bring our life dreams and visions into the world. All cultures regard the importance of vision and its capacity to magnetize the creative spirit. Shamanic societies use vision quests, extended periods of solitude in nature, as a way of remembering their life dream and of accessing the four ways of seeing: intuition, perceptions, insight, and vision.

Many Native American cultures hold a belief that each individual is "original medicine," nowhere duplicated on the planet and that therefore it is important to bring the creative spirit and life dream or purpose to Earth. Because we are "original medicine," these native people see that there is no need for comparison or competition. The work is to come forward fully with our gifts, talents and resources and to powerfully meet our tests and challenges. *The Visionary is one who brings his or her voice into the world and who refuses to edit, rehearse, perform or hide all ways we can feed the false-self system of denial and indulgence* [emphasis added]. Among some indigenous peoples, the direction of the East is associated with the home of the Great Spirit, the place of the rising sun and the place where we come home to our authentic self. Archetypically, the bell or conch shell serves as a sonic voice that calls people together and calls us as individuals to remember our authentic purpose.

The human resource of vision is the container that magnetizes the creative spirit to bring one's original medicine into the world. It is the Visionary within that inspires the voice to share what it sees. Rollo May states what shamanic traditions have practiced for centuries, "If you do not express your own original ideas, if you do not listen to your own being, you will have betrayed yourself."*

I am paraphrasing Angeles Arrien when I say, "How do we know everybody is in the place they're supposed to be?" Well, the answer is, because they're there. How do we know that what's supposed to be happening is happening? Because it's happening. If we want things to be different, creatively, we have to envision them and *make* them different.

People who overidentify with the upper three chakras may spout all kinds of wonderful idealistic possibilities that everyone, everywhere would all love to see manifest in our world. These heady visions might make us feel high and good until we finally come to realize that the people express-

---

*Please see www.angelesarrien.com for additional information on Angeles Arrien and the four archetypes.

ing them don't have one grounded wire. It is hard to take visionaries seriously as real role models for shamanic psychospiritual integration when they aren't paying adequate attention to their human sides, when they are not being solidly reliable or accountable for the most fundamental and basic aspects of their lives and are flaky in their personal relationships.

Another issue with extremes is that if one finds oneself polarized in the light, one may suddenly swing to the dark. Conversely, if you are polarized in the lower three chakras, you might make an extreme about-face to the light. Neither one of these extremes are where we want to live our everyday lives, although it appears that all things and beings have the ability to move toward their opposite and that for a great shift to occur, extremes are sometimes necessary. The light and the dark are polar opposites, but they've got to have a *dialogue* in order for us to manifest our future selves and to bring in what we want to bring in right now so that this planet and the species here can continue to survive, so that we can continue to have a learning ground for human consciousness to evolve.

## THE YONI STAR GATE

Let's go back to our two opposing triangles for a moment. When they first meet, the very first form they create, *before* they create the six-pointed star, is a four-pointed star, or diamond shape. While the two triangles are communicating, each point—associated with the four directions of east, south, west, and north as well as the four elements of earth, water, air, and fire—is undergoing an alchemical transformation. The connection of the four elements and the four directions reminds me of the ancient medicine wheels, but this stage of the process holds additional meaning. The two triangles are forming a star portal for integrating the energies of all the chakras and elements.

This fusion of the four-pointed star activates all four of the elements needed for creation and, in so doing, become the eye of the yoni, which is a Hindu term for the vaginal opening from which all life springs. As discussed earlier in the book, I believe that at the beginning of time

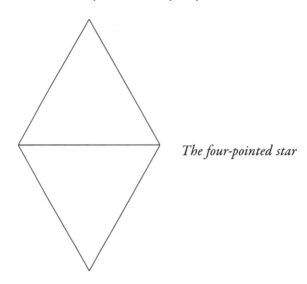

*The four-pointed star*

there was a very powerful cosmic energy of the One Source. When this One Source opened up or caused a big bang, it unfolded into the four messengers of the four neteru: water, earth, air, and fire.

The elements have existed and evolved over billions of years. Try to imagine the evolution of the elements within different solar systems, different galaxies, and different stars, and picture in your mind what life might be like in those realms. There is life as we know it, but there could be many other varieties and forms of life as well. If we travel into the deepest parts of the ocean, we will see the life forms that exist there. These are unlike any other life forms that we know. It seems impossible that they could exist in the amount of darkness and cold that they inhabit. It certainly is not life as we know it.

If we went to the very heights of the world, we would find bacteria living in an atmosphere where we couldn't possibly live. Again, this would not be life as we know it. We don't know what life looks like in other places and situations, so it is ridiculous to say, "That planet couldn't sustain life." What we're really saying is that it couldn't sustain life as we presently know it on Earth.

I often imagine the One Source in the universe longing to experience as many creative possibilities of consciousness as possible, in endless sequences of birth, death, and rebirth, and that this intense longing built up until it exploded in an orgasmic force that resulted in the four messengers that in our world have become the beautiful elemental beings of water, earth, fire, and air.

According to my vision, in ancient Egypt these four elemental beings, or messengers, were known as the sacred neteru; they were the elder gods—the oldest gods on the planet. And all the deities that came after them, such as Isis and Anubis and Osiris, were vibrational emanations of the elder gods.

Some of the earliest medicine wheels and standing stone circles of various primitive societies contain four quadrants, which represent the four elements and the four directions. The horizontal and vertical arms of the Christian cross and the Celtic cross make up the four directions. Many years ago, I learned from an indigenous teacher that in the Catholic Church, when you make the sign of the cross and only honor the Trinity—the Father, Son, and Holy Ghost—you are not honoring the quadrinity most often associated with the older religions that came long before those of the present day.

In this, the earthier element of the feminine in the genuflection was completely left out. In omitting this (human power, dark power, earth power), not only was women's power diminished, but also diminished were the powerful creative feminine aspects within us all.

What the Catholic Church *didn't* say when they left off the fourth element from the Trinity, was that they cut off the Great Goddess and left her out of the spiritual equation. What was left was the Father, Son, and Holy Spirit instead of *Mother,* Father, Son, and Holy Spirit. The indigenous people of the world, even going back into Neolithic times when people were drawing sacred images upon cave walls, knew about and acknowledged these four primary energies.

They frequently drew a circle with the cross in the center pointing in the four different directions; some referred to this as a medicine shield or a sacred hoop. The circle enclosing the four directions was often symbolic of the sacred container or the womb of the Great Mother, who held all the energies within.

When we invoke the four directions of east, south, west, and north, we are calling in powerful elemental forces of nature and the "spirit keepers" who guard or stand at each gate. Most cultures that have celebrated the sacred wheel of life have assigned an element, color, and guardian to each of the four directions. They understand that these four directions greatly influence humans on their path around the sacred wheel of life.

## THE BREATH OF GOD

In addition to the four elements, there is a fifth. The fifth element has its origins all the way back in the original spark of the One Source. This fifth element is the breath of God, or God's spirit, an ingredient necessary to impregnate and activate all the other elements. Without this spark of life-force energy coming from the original source, we would all be more akin to Frankenstein walking around without a spirit inside of us—soulless, heartless human beings.

Of course, the elements are dynamic in and of themselves, but the fifth element adds so much more. The stories of the activating energy of God or a deity breathing the sacred breath into the clay of the earth depict how these elements were animated into consciousness. This fifth element of spirit—otherwise known as pneuma, chi, or prana—when breathed into form, is activated and becomes life itself.

God's breath, if you will, is the symbol for all of life.

In my vision, the pantheon of Egyptian gods, four is the number of Khnum, the master craftsman who creates everything that is in form. The diamond or four-pointed star is also the portal for transformation between the worlds. Some associate the symbol with the Merkaba, which is a Hasidic* philosophy that seeks to guide the soul as it travels through its incarnations of experience.

---

*Hasidism was founded by Rabbi Israel Baal Shem Tov in the eighteenth century in Eastern Europe. It is a branch of Judaism that, while acknowledging the importance of studying the Torah, emphasizes and encourages its members to seek unity with God by concentrating and focusing on God throughout the course of one's daily life, in all its aspects.

The Merkaba is a Hasidic analogy to the neteru. It is a chariot of ascension composed of four angels, which symbolize the forces that God used to construct our reality. Fundamentally its symbols are the lion, representing fire; the ox, earth; the man, water; and the eagle, air. These four elements may also represent the four seasons.

Overseeing these four elements is humanity, which represents an all-seeing, all-knowing God, completely in control of how the four elements act and interact in harmony with one another. The fact that they are in harmony implies the existence of a God who can and does harmonize all of the differences that exist between them. If there were no harmony, God would not be present.

The philosophy behind the Merkaba indicates that humanity, acting in a similar capacity to God orchestrating the spiritually harmonizing activities of humankind, should try to realize and integrate all of its talents, with the goal in so doing to please God and to follow God's will.

## THE SIX-POINTED STAR

Once we move decisively into the symbolism of the four, we activate the heart chakra. As the two triangles of the upper and lower chakras come together and the heart is activated, the two triangles begin to merge.

As they enter into one another and reach their rightful position, these two triangles form the beautiful six-pointed star, also known as the Star of David. I call it the Blue Star Shamanic Wheel of Transformation, or the Blue Star Wheel, for short. Grandma Twylah talked about star energy and the Great Star Nation of harmony and balance. Six is the number of reconciliation, the number of forgiveness; it's the number that truly tells us that the two triangles have now come together in complete integration.

In *The Anubis Oracle* book and deck, the number six is associated with Sobek and Horus. Sobek represents the more restrictive older evo-

*The six-pointed star with the heart intact*

lutionary patterns that are part of who we "have been." Horus, on the other hand, is the young god who represents a new and expanded way of being. Their challenge and purpose is to bring together the opposite energies and to create a divine third. In other words, they must reconcile their differences and achieve forgiveness, unity, and understanding with each other so that they may co-create something of beauty in the world that possesses a portion of both their qualities.

In creating the six-pointed star, we have moved from two separate energies of three to one unified energy of four, and now to the integrative energy of six. You will notice that through this shamanic psychospiritual journey of merging the opposites, all the opposing points add up to eight. Chakras one and seven add up to eight, three and five add up to eight, and two and six add up to eight.

## THE ENERGETIC SIGNIFICANCE OF "EIGHT"

Eight is the number I associated with the Egyptian goddess Ma'at, who brings us her qualities of harmony, truth, radiance, and balance. Each of the chakras has its own energy, but when we balance them in this way, with the sum total being eight, we achieve a shamanic psychospiritual integration, also known as a sacred union or a sacred marriage of the human and the divine. Thus we arrive at a highly charged and integrated state—some might even call it a state of enlightenment.

The magician's symbol, called a lemniscate (which we mentioned briefly earlier) looks like a figure eight lying on its side. It also looks like two loops that cross over, and it is often referred to as the infinity symbol. This represents the energy of all of us as we travel back and forth and back and forth between the worlds of form and formlessness. If we keep the energy moving, then there's a free-flowing and easy communion between the spirit and the human as they make friends and harmonize and blend with each other instead of remaining separate and polarized.

*The concept of infinity, denoted by the lemniscate*

In medieval times, eternity was symbolized by the Ouroboros serpent, a snake devouring its own tail. This imagery was also expressed as a lizard or a dragon. In ancient Egypt and Greece, it was understood as that which is constantly being devoured and then reborn—energy never dies; it just changes form.

Even though the symbolism of numbers and figures might seem esoteric, understanding their practical meaning can be useful for our everyday lives. We harmonize the energies of the first chakra (Earth/

*The Ouroboros, symbol of the empty circle of eternity*

root) with those of the seventh chakra (Heaven), and in so doing we create the state of consciousness known as "on Earth as it is in Heaven," or "as above, so below." In bringing the energies of the second chakra (our sexual energy and creative urges) into harmony with the sixth chakra (our highest vision and insight), we are able to manifest our ideas and our ideals in the world. And in bringing the energies of the third chakra (our soul's power) into alignment with the energies of the fifth chakra (authentic expression), we create an outer expression that has dignity and integrity.

These chakras without their counterparts—one and seven, two and six, or three and five—are out of balance, and always the fourth chakra, which is the energy of the One Source and our own heart, brings them together. If we blocked out the heart connection in the center of the symbol, there wouldn't be a way to connect the points between the pairs of chakras. There would be no real connection or relationship.

Now let's put the heart back in, bringing us back to our three eights, with the four in the middle. If you want to increase the potency and vibration of this symbol even further, then add the heart chakra number four to each of the opposing chakras that added up to eight, and you will get the number twelve. The number twelve has had a lot of special mystical significance throughout history (which is too detailed to go into here).

In *The Anubis Oracle* deck, the Enlightened Heart Shaman Anubis navigates the portal between the worlds; his number is twelve in the oracle deck. Twelve is the symbolic number for the shamanic being who

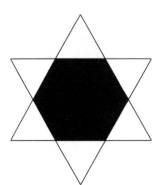

*The six-pointed star without the energy of the heart*

has the ability to walk between the diverse worlds of one and seven, two and six, and three and five. He is able to travel to all the worlds because his heart is awakened, enlightened, and wide open.

Ma'at's energy of truth, the eight, is constantly balancing us, and when you add the number four, we become Anubis, number twelve, the shaman with the enlightened heart who is capable of bringing Heaven to Earth.

The sum of the three eights we get from matching the counterparts of all the chakras to one another equals twenty-four. If we reduce twenty-four to its base number, it becomes six $(2 + 4 = 6)$. So again we have the energy of six, of reconciliation and forgiveness, at play.

The energy of eight is an extremely dynamic place; we can work toward spending more time in the field of that energy in our daily lives. It's not to say that even if we strive to attain it, we're going to achieve that truth and harmony and radiance and balance every day. No, we're not always going to be in that perfect six-pointed star. The six-pointed star is a potent symbol for humanity, much like the medicine wheel, the peace symbol, or the cross. It's a symbol that we look to as a reminder to stay in this energy more often and to come back to this energy over and over again so that we can remember who we are while we're in form.

## THE DANCE BETWEEN PAST AND FUTURE

Currently on the planet, we spend a lot of time in the lower chakras. Now, the lower chakras aren't bad except if they are not processed through the heart. Then they become destructive. You just wouldn't shoot somebody if your heart was connected to your feelings, your thoughts, and your actions. You would know that you were shooting some mother's child, and you would feel like you were shooting your own child or like you were shooting yourself, because at a core level we are related to the One Source and truly are all one.

We wouldn't do some of the things we do if our hearts were open. However, we're an evolving species, and at some level, part of the plan is to be allowed to make mistakes and even to mis-create so that we can learn the true nature of power and explore the mystery school of good and evil, dark and light. Then, when we begin to create consciously, we will stop creating from insanity and begin to create with awareness and with a connection to all living things.

Symbolic Mayan art often depicts two spirals, one going counterclockwise and one going clockwise. When you're practicing Shamanic Reiki or other systems of energy healing, you will frequently encounter energy symbols that run counterclockwise to unlock things and then run clockwise to move things forward. In this respect, one spiral represents working with things from the past—even though the past has already happened—and the other spiral involves working with energies that exist in the future.

Likewise, when we do breathwork, we're either spinning backward in our spiral of transformation or spinning forward into the future. We're either healing the past or we're learning about the future and perhaps calling in our imaginal cells. Sometimes we do both at the same time. We may experience a void time, a period when we feel like nothing is happening, but that may be a time of deep healing or of receiving big downloads from the imaginal worlds.

When we're engaged in energy healing, we're clearing up the past and calling in the future; we're working with those two spirals, backward and forward, and we're doing it in the present. We're becoming the Aquarian Visionary shaman, standing in between the worlds, shapeshifting our lives, weaving the future and healing the past so that we can be more potent and powerful in the present. We can *experience* all of this and more through Shamanic Breathwork and other new paradigm methods that help us to travel spiritually as well as psychologically. We can gain a clearer understanding of the energies of our lives through the visual images and activation that the sacred geometry of shamanic psychospiritual transformation freely offers up to us.

# 11
# STAR WOLF'S PERSONAL ENCOUNTER WITH ISIS

*To every thing there is a season, and a time to every purpose under the heaven: a time to be born, and a time to die; a time to plant, and a time to pluck up that which is planted; a time to kill, and a time to heal; a time to break down, and a time to build up; a time to weep, and a time to laugh; a time to mourn, and a time to dance; a time to cast away stones, and a time to gather stones together; a time to embrace, and a time to refrain from embracing; a time to get, and a time to lose; a time to keep, and a time to cast away; a time to rend, and a time to sew; a time to keep silence, and a time to speak; a time to love, and a time to hate; a time of war, and a time of peace.*

ECCLESIASTES 3:1

In 2009 I had an extremely powerful shamanic vision with Isis during an intense Shamanic Breathwork journey. Some readers may not be familiar with her, so I will tell her story as I understand it. In ancient Egypt there was one who loved unconditionally and who "remembered" the beloved, and her name was Isis. One of the greatest shamanic love stories of all time is the story of Isis and Osiris. Many variations of this story have been passed down through the ages. This one is mine.

## FOR THE LOVE OF ISIS

Isis represents the great wise queen—the holy mother of all. It is said that all beings were born from her, and she gave them her unconditional love. She was the original mother; some think of her as a prototype for Mother Nature or Mother Nurture. Osiris, her husband and lover, was the great lord of the land; he represents the death of the old and the regeneration into a new birth. He was also the lord of all living, growing things, and as such, he was an emanation of the original vegetation god, also known as the Green Man. He loved his kingdom and the sacred Nile valley, which he served and tended very well.

Because of his great love and nurturance for all living things, he also knew when it was time for things to die so that they might be regenerated and become new again, for as it says in biblical scripture "to everything there is a season." This is the regenerative principle inside each one of us. We can look at the changes we each need to make as being caused by external events, or we can perceive them internally as archetypes or principles that have been activated and are calling fate to us.

Isis and Osiris were great lovers and partners who walked on this planet as archetypal beings demonstrating the principles of unconditional love and regeneration after death. For a time they lived in a kind of idyllic perfection that was similar to the Garden of Eden.

Then came a time when the shadow arose, as it always seems to do when the season calls it forth. Who knows why it arises? Maybe in all creation there has to be the dark as well as the light in order for things to be renewed. This great shadow was called Set, and he was Osiris's brother. Some say he became jealous of Osiris and Isis and their beautiful kingdom. Set and his wife, Nephthys, lived in the hot, fiery desert, where he ruled his kingdom as a fierce and mighty warrior.

One day Set threw a party for Osiris and said to him, "I have created a beautiful sarcophagus for you, and someday when you pass you will be buried with honor in it. Why don't you lie down in it now so I can see if it's the right size?" At that point, I think if I were Osiris I might have suspected something funny. However, he didn't or—perhaps knowing intuitively that this was part of his journey—he did.

In any event, when Osiris got into the sarcophagus, Set had his henchmen quickly close the lid and throw it into the river. Isis soon realized that her beloved was missing and began to search. Meanwhile, Osiris floated down the Nile until finally he came to a bank upon which grew a great tamarisk tree. The sarcophagus became ensconced in this magnificent tree, which is also a symbol for the Tree of Life.

Isis was so distressed that she pulled her hair out and tore at her clothes as she set out to find her soul mate. She looked for him everywhere. The whole time she was grieving deeply and in despair, which was appropriate to the situation. It is entirely appropriate to feel grief, loss, difficulty, and struggle around change because those feelings are an important part of the entire spiraling death and rebirth process.

Isis knew that she must find Osiris. She knew that he held the sacred keys to immortality, the regenerative principle of life and death. She knew that without his energy she would not be able to fully re-create life in the world. She traveled to another kingdom where—lo and behold!— she found a great temple, one of the pillars of which had been made out of the same tamarisk tree that Osiris was lying dormant inside of.

To be close to her husband, Isis took a position as a governess in the household of the king who ruled over the temple, without revealing her true identity. In this role, she oversaw the care of the king and queen's child. Here again we are faced with a metaphor: this time one of youth and the principle of regeneration.

Isis was a mistress of magic. Every night, unbeknownst to the royal household, she worked her enchantment, which in this case consisted of putting the child over the fire and appearing to roast it. Now, this might seem an abomination, but in reality, she was "tempering" the child. Why? In life, we undergo shamanic trials by fire, and by being put in the flames again and again, we become tempered and resilient. Isis teaches us how to go through the various fires of transformation without being consumed by the powerful flames. She teaches us to remember who we are at our vibral core even while we are dissolving into mush.

Isis is busy working her alchemical magic upon the child one evening when the king and queen come in. They scream when they see what she is doing to their royal offspring. At this point Isis rises up as her true magnificent self and reveals her real identity to them. She also imparts the whole story of her husband, including the fact that Osiris has ended up as one of the pillars of their temple. The king and queen are sympathetic to her plight, and they give the pillar to her. She removes the sarcophagus from the pillar and takes Osiris back home to the sacred isle of Philae. There she summons her twin sister, Nephthys, to seek her assistance in helping to awaken Osiris.

Some call Nephthys the veiled Isis, the mysterious one who is behind the scenes. Isis is the outer mistress of magic in the world, penetrating it with her great love, but Nephthys is the mistress of magic who lives behind the veil. She represents the deeply intuitive part of us, the part that understands the mysteries and sends all the information through to our conscious mind. Her husband, Set, is both the brother of Osiris as well as his executioner. Set represents the shadow, and both he and Nephthys may be seen as the lunar or darker counterparts of Osiris and Isis.

Isis needs big magic for what she's about to do, so she calls in powerful reinforcements from her sister Nephthys. They begin the magic ceremony by placing Osiris onto a solid stone bier. Isis spins and spirals until she becomes a white kite (a small white hawk), while Nephthys holds the space, offering up songs and incantations to encourage the Great Mystery to reveal its secrets.

Isis's great love and determination, along with the magic of the ceremony, bring up the life-force energy within her. This powerful surge awakens the dormant life-force energy of Osiris, which rises up as well, manifested in his phallic energy, which Isis then descends to meet. As she joins with her husband and their life-force energies unite, she becomes impregnated with their son, Horus, the hawk-headed one. He is to become the new king, the new pharaoh.

There is a lot more to this story, but the most important part to keep in mind is that Isis is the one who remembers us no matter what happens in our lives. She is the one who loves us unconditionally and ensures that our connection to the Great Mystery is strong. Her energy is the One Source implanted within our vibral core that never forgets who we are and never forgets that on the other side of death is rebirth. She will go to any lengths to reconnect us to Osiris, the regenerative energy, and remind us how to bring forth the life-force energy over and over again, through all the cycles of change, through all the shamanic processes of life, death, and rebirth.

We can't ever be lost because Isis, our true mother, remembers where we are on our journey. She never loses her children; she never loses what she loves. She knows how to find them and bring them back to life. She brings back the life-force energy and impregnates herself through this energy, through her union with her counterpart, her beloved. She is impregnated with what is to become the new king, the new pharaoh. This new power in the world is personified as masculine energy in this archetypal story, but really it's more about our phallic, yang, or outer energy.

We use the terms *masculine* and *feminine,* but this polarity represents a fairly new outlook. While our respective genders may be feminine or masculine, our soul nature is androgynous. Over time and through cultural need perhaps, many cultures have assigned certain tasks to women and certain tasks to men, and by calling things masculine or feminine, we further solidify these distinctions. Many of us who have the eyes to see and ears to hear notice that many women have a lot of qualities typically ascribed to men and vice-versa. In point of fact, we're all a combination of masculine and feminine, or what I prefer to call yin and yang. The yin energy is a more receptive, internal, and receiving kind of energy, and the yang energy is more active, phallic, and projecting.

Isis is truly a combination of both the yin and the yang energies. She is both the Great Mother of us all, Mother Nature holding everything in her arms—she's got the whole world in her hands, or under her wings—and at the same time very powerful and directive, or phallic. By conjuring up the life-force energy, she is the proactive visionary shaman who knows how to activate regeneration with her own shakti energy.

While lying dormant and receptive in the sarcophagus, Osiris is in a disintegration phase, like the caterpillar in the cocoon, readying himself for his next incarnation. He undergoes a sort of transmutation and is being slowly renewed so that he will be able to impregnate Isis with a new power that is coming into the world—as represented by their son, Horus.

Horus was born with a human body like his father. His head, however, is that of a hawk with an all-seeing eye. This gave him clarity of vision, which he inherited from his mother. Isis is known for her ability to enter a magical trance state, and she always looks out over the world with unconditional love. And, like Isis, Horus can rise up and fly over his kingdom, gaining an expanded view that reveals what is truly going on in his world.

Later, the tale of Isis and Osiris evolved into a variety of shamanic stories in the Greek, Roman, Judeo-Christian, and Arthurian mythologies. These powerful archetypes are real psychic principles, whether you believe they exist or not. They are retold throughout history whenever they are needed. The principles of remembrance and regeneration are so powerful that they are eternal hopes we carry within ourselves. They are reflected in the ability to re-create ourselves time and again and in the dream of achieving immortal life on Earth or in the hereafter.

When Brad and I visited Egypt in 2005, we went to Isis's inner sanctuary and temple on the Isle of Philae. It was Brad's fiftieth birthday, and he led a ceremony in honor of Isis that day. Together with a breathwork group of almost forty people, we arrived at the temple in the wee hours of the morning when no one else was there except the temple guards. With a special pass that Nicki Scully had procured, we entered this amazing, sacred place after our ceremony in the Holy of Holies and walked through the courtyard to an open pavilion, where we all participated in a group meditation and Shamanic Breathwork journey.

On this day we asked Isis to come forward to activate and raise our life-force energies and implant within us the Osirian powers of regeneration. Our group, called the "As One" group (a word play on the Egyptian place-name Aswan), breathed on this pavilion by the water as the sun rose high in the sky. As we performed the ceremony, scores of little white birds—one of Isis's representations—flew around the temple. Many in the group felt it was the most memorable event of our entire trip.

## SEKHMET'S TRANSFORMATION

In 2009, I had another very powerful encounter with Isis while I was doing a breathwork session high up in the magical blue mountains of North Carolina, right above Cherokee land. During this breathwork journey I found myself upon a precipice overlooking what at first seemed to be a forest, then the African savanna. However, I quickly realized that my sight was unlimited. From where I stood, I could see in all four directions of the earth. I looked out over the desert, the mountains, the oceans, the forest, the high plateaus, and the plains—but no matter where I looked I saw massive destruction of the land and everything on it: the people, the animals, the plant life, and the earth itself.

I looked down at what were my lion paws, and I realized that I was in my Sekhmet lioness form, which is a form that I frequently identify with and shape-shift into during my shamanic journeys. Sekhmet is a powerful Egyptian goddess and warrioress who appears in my visions and dreams as a spirit guide when transformation is needed. I see her as the one who helps to transform the world through her fierce compassion. She is the embodiment of the spiritual warrior, and her main function is to bring healing and transformation not only to individuals but to the whole planet. She refuses to allow us to remain the same when change is called for in our lives.

Her ferocity, determination, and compassion drive her forward. She is loyal to the truth and serves the higher self on its evolutionary journey of manifesting its sacred purpose. However, she must be careful of her own shadow, which is to blindly push ahead—no matter the cost—toward what she believes to be the correct outcome. I say this because at times even Sekhmet, the spiritual warrior, must surrender and allow a power greater than her own to emerge. This even-greater function could be called grace, or unconditional love.

I could feel Sekhmet's familiar power and strength within my body and spirit, but when I looked out upon the world through her great eyes, I suddenly felt very small and helpless, and I despaired. Initially, in my breathwork vision, I allowed the rage to burst forth as I thrashed about and tried to stop the ravaging of the planet. I endlessly searched the rivers and streams, trying to find just one fish to eat that didn't have mercury poisoning. I witnessed whole majestic mountaintops being blasted apart for their coal and minerals. I cried huge tears as great trees were burned and rain forests clear-cut, leaving only desolation upon the land.

My heart felt as if it would break as I witnessed child soldiers, no older than ten or eleven years of age, killing people, not only in third-world countries, but in the ghettos of modern towns and cities of the United States and across the planet. The whole world was in utter chaos and fear, and apathy, bitterness, and greed ran rampant in the hearts of all people everywhere.

I felt myself losing control as I raged, frothing at the mouth and tearing things up as I whirled in pain and confusion. I fought, I roared, I slashed out wildly with my mighty claws. I ran in all directions trying to stop the killing, stop the destruction, all the while with hot tears streaming down my face, and all to no avail. I felt so discouraged, as if my life and everything I had done on my spiritual path to avert the destruction of the planet and humankind had all been for naught. I fell to the ground in a hopeless slump and curled up weeping, silently preparing to die.

At the moment when I finally felt that I had completely surrendered by realizing that all I had ever done or could do would never be enough to prevent or stop the suffering and insanity of this world, I felt myself being lifted up as tears ran down my lioness cheeks. Very slowly I noticed that I was being held in the arms of some great being or force, and I was afraid. I could not imagine what could have the strength to hold me and my anger, my fear, and my despair.

When I found the courage and the willingness to raise my head, I found myself looking into the face of the most beautiful goddess I have even seen. She had a magnificent headdress of curved golden horns upon her head, with a reddish golden orb in the middle of those powerful horns and a silver cobra snake with a flared neck encircling her head. Her hair was inky black and her eyes sparkled as they changed from dark green to deep, dark black blue, then sky blue, and then golden amber brown. Her skin was as creamy white as the Milky Way itself, and she was truly the most beautiful, powerful woman I have ever seen.

She seemed amused at my awe of her, and she smiled as I stared at her in wonder. I thought that I must have regressed into a small baby lion in order for her to be able to hold me in such a manner, because I was lying across her arms and felt so tiny and helpless in comparison to her. As she read my thoughts, she gently started laughing, as I had not registered who she was yet. Suddenly, with a bit of a shock, I realized that this was the magnificent Holy Mother Goddess, Queen of Us All! This was none other than Isis, the pure embodiment of unconditional love. My true mother!

She held me, a full-grown lion—no, wait . . . ! I had somehow shapeshifted (much to my dismay) into a tiger! I didn't want to be a tiger. My identity was tied to being the lioness and having Sekhmet's powers of transformation. What was happening to me? I didn't know anything about being a tiger. I felt angry again. Her mind connected with mine, and I was told that I was evolving more into her likeness and that the tiger stripes resembled her striped, fantastic, multicolored wings. She laughed gently and called me daughter.

Even though Isis was such a huge, overpowering presence and I was so small, I came to understand that she was holding me in this way because I was her beloved child. Even so, in my distress, I said through my tears of pain and shame, "All I have ever done to try to make a difference on this Earth has been in vain. My life has been a waste, and I have been very foolish."

Her steady gaze then pierced into my soul as she quietly but firmly said, "No, this is not the case. Even if the world as we know it ended at this very moment due to those who have refused to wake up, and ignorance and greed continue to ravage this planet, no acts done in my name, in the name of love, are *ever* wasted—regardless of what happens during the turning of the spiral wheel of creation, destruction, and regeneration. The joy that comes from healing and transformation is just as real as the destruction and despair. They are each a counterpart to one another and make up the great dance of life, death, and rebirth upon this plane of existence.

"This is one of the greatest lessons and initiations of this level of consciousness. The love you experience and share in your simple everyday actions is real. The energy of love lives forever in the spirits of all those it touches, regardless of the fate that awaits this world or any other throughout eternity. The thing you have misunderstood about your sacred purpose is that it has never been about saving others or the planet, but about evolving consciousness, which is synonymous with opening yourself to love. You have certainly accomplished that many times in your life and work, as have others who share the same dream."

I took in her words and then, still feeling saddened by all that I had envisioned, I said, "So is it too late to turn the spiral wheel one more time before we perish and the human experiment has failed?"

This time she heaved a sigh and said the following words, very simply, "Weep not, be angry not, my beloved daughter, pride of Sekhmet, lineage of Hathor. Go now and build five altars—temples for me—and I will do the rest."

I didn't know what to say. I hesitated and she repeated, "Build five altars upon this Earth to hold the four messengers of Heaven and Earth and their origin, the One Source. First, build the temple of spirit, then of fire, then of earth and air and water. If you make this commitment, all else will unfold as it should."

I looked at her with disbelief, and she said again, "You do this and I will do the rest." When I asked her what she meant, she patiently smiled and repeated the words, "Do your part and trust me to do the rest."

As I took in all that she said, I realized that, even in the totality of the moment, I was not able to fully trust, and I simply could not commit to her request. I still felt too overwhelmed, and I reeled from the wide range of feelings that had overtaken me from all the pain and suffering I witnessed in the destruction of world during my breathwork vision. It was too real and too devastating for me, and I felt defeated. I wept silently in shame in her great arms and all was quiet.

Again, I would like to reference Mellen-Thomas Benedict because one of his revelations during his near-death experience paralleled mine. Prior to Mellen-Thomas's "death," he had become distraught over the way that we human beings are destroying each other and our planet, but he was shown, as Isis showed me, that all of the calamities that have happened have served to bring humankind together by raising our collective consciousness.

## BREAKDOWNS AND BREAKTHROUGHS

I came out of the breathwork session with Isis feeling overwhelmed with all my myriad thoughts and emotions from what I had both witnessed and experienced. Thank Goddess that I have been through the five cycles of change on this spiral path enough to at least have an inkling that I might be in a process of change—of the death and rebirth of some aspect of my consciousness. I knew this was not a mere fantasy but a real scene from within what is not only my own consciousness, but the collective consciousness, and it was going to take a much larger force than any of our ego agendas, mine or anyone else's, to turn this sinking Earth ship around in the middle of the cosmic ocean.

Even if it does eventually sink, there is still a sacred purpose for all of us who choose to "grow up" into the likeness of our creator and claim our true heritage and soul powers. The human experiment has always been about evolving toward our god-self about embodying spirit in matter, and we have already been through many turns of the wheel, with civilizations rising and falling repeatedly. We are at a time of breakdown on our planet; we have reached the tipping point. The good news is that breakdowns always precede breakthroughs.

This breakdown is a psychic experience that lives inside each of us, and as such, we each will experience it differently. But the fact remains that each one of us is being called. When we are finally able to surrender the ego's control over our spiritual essence and allow grace (which is love unearned and freely given) to enter our lives, we are uplifted and transformed into something bigger. Consequently, we are asked to give up self-seeking, which never really satisfied our constant hunger and longing anyway. We are asked to enter into that bigger story as real players instead of sitting on the sidelines of life, waiting for someone or something to rescue us.

The wounded little child in each of us may have a hard time making this reach. We certainly need to take care of that wounded child and to listen to its fears, its ranting and raving as it throws a temper tantrum, much like I did in my breathwork session. But that child was never meant to be in charge of our adult lives, or the world. As spiritual beings we can reclaim our spiritual powers and step into our soul's purpose, which changes as we shape our consciousness through every choice, through every step we take.

## SHARING THE VISION

Over the next week as I went about my business—teaching my workshops, traveling to Vermont to meet with my publishers and offer a one-day Shamanic Breathwork session there—I kept hearing Isis's words, "Do your part and I will do the rest." Part of me still felt overwhelmed and resistant to this, as if perhaps I might still have a choice not to do as she requested.

When I came home from New England, Brad could tell I was feeling "stuck in the muck" and that I needed to do some more Shamanic Breathwork. I breathed for about twenty minutes or so while he helped me move metaphorically through the birth canal and fully emerge into the fire cycle of transformation. As my vision cleared and I had the sensation that at least my head was out of the cosmic birth canal, I had the body-felt sense that I was a daughter of a goddess, of Isis. I am growing one day at a time into her likeness, acknowledging her attributes that wish to come forward in my own life more fully.

I am also a kindred sister of Sekhmet, the Spiritual Warrior Lioness. My destiny, if I choose it, is to grow up in the likeness of my divine relationships, the archetypes of my soul. The time is here and the time is now—at least for me. If I truly want to be happy, at peace, and on purpose, then I must do my part by trusting my path and letting go of judgment and final outcomes. No more waiting!

A few days later I breathed yet again. This time I saw myself as a tiger woman who had become a queen. As such, I was able to witness the regeneration of the planet; the animals, trees, mountains, and streams were all coming back to life as I stepped off an iceberg and onto a greening shoreline of beauty. I had a real sense of stepping into my power as Isis emanated her energies of love and queenly wisdom through me for all of her creatures and beings upon the planet. I knew I had finally accepted the Great Mystery's divine plan for my life—for my little part of evolution. I knew that I would do what Isis had asked of me, with gratitude, fully releasing all expectations and opening to all the love that I am to give and receive along the way.

Since that time, with inspiration from kindred spirits, we have created three of the five temples here at Isis Cove Retreat Center, fulfilling visions that were received in shamanic encounters with Isis. The Blue Star Spirit Deck on top of Dove Mountain, the Medicine Wheel Earth Altar, and the Fire Portal Altar have been completed; the Air Temple is under way; and the Water Temple is yet to be built. Venus Rising University for Shamanic Psychospiritual Studies (founded on August 6, 2010) utilizes each of the temples as sacred places, as well as classrooms for learning, healing, and celebration.

# 12

# SHAMANIC TOOLS FOR LEARNING FROM THE FUTURE

*Isis* is that principle that says "Everything that we need, we already have." When we reflect on the atrocities happening on our planet—the wars raged in Iraq, Afghanistan, and Pakistan; the homelessness and the hunger; poverty and widespread disease; and the collective trauma that all of this causes—we have to know that no matter what's happened to us in this world, whether by fate or accident or perpetration, we can regenerate our bodies, our minds, our emotions, and our spirits.

Perhaps we're frustrated because we're not in right relationship to our work in the world, or perhaps we're suffering from some horrible loss or wound, or maybe we have an addiction that we can't get rid of. Whatever the burden, we have to know that we don't have to be stuck eternally in our predicament—not in this life. We can regenerate; we can die and we can be reborn.

This is the heart and soul of shamanic psychospiritual teachings, and this is the heart and soul of the cycles of change. This is really the hope, the deep inner knowing, and the remembrance that we have. It's part of what we need to become to be the change we want to see in the world.

## THE SPIDER'S MESSAGE

Who needs to change? Well, I can look around and tell you I think *you* need to change, but I also know that change must begin within my own heart first. I am the one who needs to change.

A few years ago at the Wise Wolf Women's Council, an annual gathering of women cofounded by me and my shamanic sister Amai Clarice Munchus-Bullock that is held at Isis Cove, a spider bit me. When I was getting into our hot tub after a full day, I noticed a sting on my hip. I thought I had somehow pinched my skin on the side of the tub. It's probably a really good thing that I then got into the water because it was so hot that no doubt it pulled out a lot of the spider's venom.

My colleague Laura Wolf joined me in the tub, and we spent the next hour or two talking, until we were wizened and looked like a couple of prunes. When I got out I went straight to bed and right to sleep. I hadn't realized that I had been bitten by a spider, but oddly enough that night I dreamt of Grandmother Neith, an Egyptian deity who has appeared in my shamanic visions in many different forms. In my dream she appeared to me as a huge brown widow spider. At that point in time, I didn't even know that brown widow spiders existed. She showed up as the crone of legend, that archetype of the wise old woman, but in spider form.

I had seen her in a vision before, as a black spider at night who cast her web across the sky, catching and upholding all the starry constellations. In *Vermeer's Hat,* a history book written by Timothy Brook, the author employs a like metaphor. "Buddhism uses a similar image to describe the interconnectedness of all phenomena. It is called Indra's Net. When Indra fashioned the world, he made it as a web, and at every knot in the web is tied a pearl. Everything that exists, or has ever existed, every idea that can be thought about, every datum that is true—every dharma, in the language of Indian philosophy—is a pearl in Indra's net. Not only is every pearl tied to every other pearl by virtue of the web on which they hang, but on the surface of every pearl is reflected every other jewel on the net. Everything that exists in Indra's web implies all else that exists."

In the *Shamanic Mysteries of Egypt,* the spider that is Grandmother Neith holds the web of energies of the Great Star Nations in her legs. When I saw the spider in my dream, even though she appeared as a huge crone, a form unlike any I had experienced before, I knew she was Grandmother Neith. She was busy weaving her web and walking around doing various things when she caught me looking at her. She glared at me with very red eyes. "What?!" she demanded indignantly. Her eyes pierced into me and I felt intimidated, so much so that I didn't know if what I was experiencing was a dream or a nightmare.

It was a lucid dream, though, so I knew it was important, and I asked if she had something to tell me. She replied, "I'm here to tell you information that everyone on the planet needs to know, that everything people need is within them. They have every single thing they need to create their life any way they want to." She conveyed this to me through mental telepathy.

And I said, "Well, I don't know if that's possible because so many have a little and so few have a lot." She replied, "That's a misperception." Then she added, "You're not getting this . . . Watch!" And she proceeded to spin her beautiful, gigantic web, and it spanned the whole universe. "This is the web of life, and everything is in this web," she told me. "You already have everything that you need; the water, the earth, the air, and the fire belong equally to everyone. And no one can buy it because it's not for sale."

"But people are overusing the resources," I informed her.

"You're still not getting it," she replied. "They belong to everyone, and people have forgotten and become victims because of what's happened on the planet. Watch this." She pulled a long string of stuff out of her old body to show me; she had used this string to create the web.

"See, it comes from within you. You have it inside you all the time. Now watch what it can do. Are you hungry?" At that very moment a big fat June bug flew into her web. Nodding her head at the bug, she asked me, "Would you like some?" I tried not to recoil and simply said, "No thanks. Not right now. Maybe later."

After she finished catching many different things, I was in awe of her ability to attract to her web just what she needed. "That's amazing," I told her. "Yeah," she said. "But I didn't really want all this stuff." So she took some things out of the web and kept the things she wanted. All of a sudden a big wind came up. Looking into the sky, she murmured, "Uh oh, a storm is brewing," and she tucked away a few things to eat later. She kicked out all the other stuff and kind of shook the web, and then she took the long sticky strands back into her body.

She crawled off toward some thick bushes and trees that would protect her from the rain and re-created her web again. She turned and told me, "See, wherever I go, I have my home and everything I need to create my life. I put up my web, and I attract a lot of things, and what I don't want I shake out. No big deal."

She conveyed all this to me, and it was very powerful. And then she said, "All of you human beings are my grandchildren, and you all have the ability to do this." At that moment I remembered the Hopi myths of the Spider Grandmother, who was said to have created the world and even language. I realized that the creator spider of many spiritual traditions was an aspect of the Great Mother, just in another form, represented by a different archetype.

The next morning, lying in bed, I thought, *Oh my God, what a powerful dream. It must be from all the energy of the men and women who are at the Wise Wolf Women's Council.* I got up and felt a little hot, a little feverish, but I didn't think too much of it. I got dressed and went about my morning. That afternoon, when I had a chance to relax, I told my friend Judy Red Hawk about my powerful dream.

Just then, I felt a hot spot on my hip, which I began to scratch. When I looked down, I saw a large red welt and simultaneously had a flash of insight: I knew I had not been bitten by just any old normal spider—I had been bitten by Grandmother Neith herself.

My dream had been about a brown widow spider, which resembled a black widow spider, so I went to my computer and googled that phrase. As it turns out, although brown widow spiders are mainly found in more southerly states like Alabama, they also are known to exist in North Carolina where I live.

Although I didn't see the spider that bit me, I intuitively knew that it was a brown widow. The website showed a picture of a brown widow spider's bite. It resembled a bull's eye, which my bite was like, except that mine, oddly enough, was in the shape of a heart.

Obviously I survived the encounter with the spider, but the synchronicity of my dream with the actual bite really forced me to pay attention to the dream's message: everything that we need to heal and regenerate is within us. When I remember that, I remember something else: *Because* I have a shamanic spirit, I don't need to look outside myself for someone else to be the shaman and fix me. That's not to say that I might not want to have someone give me a lovely massage or an acupuncture treatment, or that I might not get confused for a little while and need someone to hold space for me while I get back on track.

Ultimately, even Western medical doctors know they don't heal us. They might sew us up, they might take a ruptured organ out of us, they might prescribe a medication, but they are not the healers; the healer is within. It is our mind/body that says heal. Last year, while visiting California, I spoke with Lee Lipsenthal, a friend and colleague who also happens to be a medical doctor. He received a diagnosis of terminal cancer with only about a 5 percent chance of survival. He said to me and to others who knew him that all he had to do was be one of the 5 percent.

Even though he's an incredible holistic doctor himself, he chose to do a combination of allopathic and holistic medicine. This must have been a difficult choice at first, but I could sense his total surrender to whatever the process needed to be and to go wherever the journey would take him. My sense is his amazing loving attitude of grace and surrender created a powerful activation of his inner shaman, and I am pleased to report that at as I write this, he is in remission.

On the day that he and I came together for me to do hands-on healing, including breathwork and soul return, he had an incredible attitude about his illness, one of full acceptance and an inner knowing that he was capable of healing. However, he also acknowledged that because he was willing to surrender to whatever was supposed to happen, that it might in fact *be* his time to leave the planet. He is a very clear channel and a prime example of someone getting the help they need while at the same time understanding that the healer is within.

He and other doctors have said to me, "No matter what we do as doctors, if we're really honest, we know that we don't heal anybody. We may create the environment for healing to happen or help accelerate it, but we are not the healers." Lee continued in this vein:

"Our body has a huge capacity for healing itself. Our role is to let it do what it needs to do while getting mentally and emotionally quiet. I used chemo, radiation, acupuncture, and herbs, but my core healing comes from my body and soul's wisdom of how to heal. Meditation and journeying were the key healing modalities that I needed. They also primed my body to clear and heal from the chemo and radiation after they had done their job to kill the cancer cells within me."

That the healer is within is the heart and soul of our teachings at Venus Rising Association for Transformation. Sometimes we might say, "We're healers, we're teachers," but by this we mean that we help people remember who they are. Much like Isis or Grandmother Neith, we help people remember that they have the ability to heal themselves.

## ADDICTIONS AND REMEMBERING MY TRUE SELF

In my twenties I was a mental health worker. I also was a very wounded soul, an alcoholic, and extremely codependent. I thought, given my profession, that I was saving and healing people. All the therapists and counselors I knew thought that they were saving and healing people, but we were all a bunch of codependent messes.

I had some awareness about my addictions, but I was so intent on helping others that I couldn't help myself. I was devastated, then, when I realized that I needed to stop focusing on fixing everybody else and instead do what I needed to do to get my *own* act in order. When this truth became apparent to me, I felt a lot of shame and believed that no one would ever want to work with me professionally again. I was twenty-nine, I had been a counselor since I was twenty, and I didn't want anyone to know I was an alcoholic.

I decided to go to AA, and before I went to my first meeting, I practiced what I was going to say to the group. "Hello, I'm Linda, and I'm an alcoholic." That sounded fine, and I thought I would be able to say those words, no problem. I went to the meeting, and I was the last one to stand up and say something because I wanted to hear what everybody else had to say first.

Approximately thirty people were at the meeting; it was full of "respectable" people in my town, which shocked me, to say the least. I believe I was the youngest one there. When it was my turn to introduce myself, I stood up and said, "Hello, I'm Linda, and I'm *almost* an alcoholic." Everyone laughed and I was offended, and then I went on to tell them that I wasn't really an alcoholic, and I didn't really need their help; I just wanted to hear what they were saying, and I was there because I was a counselor.

Afterward, five of them came over to me and loaded me down with every piece of recovery literature that has ever been printed and every big book and every twelve-step program and every this and every that related to recovery. And I said, "Thank you. I'll give this to someone who really needs it." And I went home and I didn't go back. I didn't go back for at least a year, when everything was a whole lot worse.

I'd sit down with Jack Daniels and Coca-Cola to read the literature, and I'd think to myself, *Wow, that sounds a little like me.* Then I'd read another section and think, *That sounds a lot like me.* My Big Book of

Alcoholics Anonymous wore many cigarette burns and liquor stains. It took awhile for my denial to break and for me to face that I was an alcoholic because, after all, I was a good mother, wasn't I? I compensated very well during the day. I cooked a great meal, solved everybody else's problems, and looked good on the outside.

So nobody knew, not until near the end of my drinking days.

I'm sharing all this with you because I had almost completely annihilated who I really was. It's called DENIAL for a reason. Don't Even kNow I Am Lying: lying to myself and lying to others. At first I was terribly humiliated, but then the humiliation transformed into a positive quality of humility, and then I was able to acknowledge that I had an addiction and vowed to do whatever it took to heal it. I gave up drinking and underwent a profound transformation, one that I'm extremely grateful for.

I had surrendered to being teachable, and I learned from other people's experience. I had strength and hope, but I also knew that no one else could fix me. There are people in recovery called sponsors, men and women who have been there and done that, which gives them a deep understanding of the process. My sponsors loved me as I was changing and held space for me. But they couldn't heal me. No doctor could heal me; no therapist could heal me. I had to make the choice that I wanted to live and be regenerated from within by my higher power and my future self. And I was.

Someone—Isis perhaps—remembered who I *really* was and remembered that my addiction was not me. I had it; it didn't have me. And if I *have* something, I can transform it. When I realized this, I remembered what I already knew. From that day until the writing of this book, it has been twenty-nine years since I have had a drink. All this time, I have been in a constant state of recalling those events and transforming those memories into the teachings we're discussing here.

There should be no shame attached to taking yourself apart periodically and regenerating your life into something new. If you think you have to stay on a straight path, you're going to live a very contracted, ego-based life instead of having a soul-based experience. You're not going to have the courage to take yourself apart and become your future self, to allow your imaginal cells that remember who you are behind the matrix to come in and help you remove your obstacles, transform your addictions, and develop the heart to stop being a victim of your emotions, to stop repeating the abuse patterns in your life.

You can sit in therapy for thirty-five years, and while a few things may change, you are not going to transform yourself at the core level. With therapy you'll gain a better understanding of your problems. Now forgive me if what I say is offensive. I believe that talk therapy is good and helpful, and that understanding your problems is a great step toward transforming them. However, I find myself becoming a bit like Grandmother Neith, annoyed with people who go to therapy and discuss the same old problems year after year instead of taking action to change their lives. I am equally disgusted with any therapist who allows clients to remain static for long periods of time without challenging their belief systems, while receiving a very nice paycheck for enabling them.

I have said to many clients and students over the years, "I love you, and I support you, and I will hold the space for you to change. I will be very patient as you go through your healing process, but I need to tell you that if you are unwilling to take a leap of faith to heal and transform your life, at some point I will cut you loose, because I'm not doing you any good. I'm not going to take your money, and I'm not going to be bored. If you are not ready to change, you need to release the spot you are holding so that someone who is ready to change can have it. This is my role in your life; this is how I honor who you really are. It may sound like tough love, but it's my best gift to you."

I've let people go who mainly wanted to complain, and they've gotten really angry at me. They felt that I was abandoning them, and in so doing, that I was re-creating their abuse. They went on to the next therapist and complained about me, but they often got better with their next counselor when they hit the same point again.

Because I am an agent of change, I'm not willing to hold space for people who waste my time or theirs for very long. Even a mother holds a baby in her womb for only nine months. The time comes when the mother bird says, "Fly." Any doctors, friends, partners, or therapists who keep you in a holding pattern, seeing you as a victim, are perpetrating their own codependency and yours. They may unconsciously need for you to be dependent upon them so that they can feel like they are fixing you and consequently feel better about themselves. Sad to say, but this is a rather common dilemma that many therapists, teachers, and healers find themselves in if they have not done much inner work on their path.

## LOOK WITHIN FOR THE
## TOOLS OF TRANSFORMATION

I'll tell you a story that illustrates the point that everything is within us. I was doing a book tour on the West Coast last year when a woman approached me about a private reading. She knew I was highly intuitive, and she wanted information from me: Should she stay with her husband? Should she move to a warmer and dryer climate? I told her I was leaving that afternoon for my next stop on the book tour but I would be more than happy to make a phone appointment with her, which we did.

On the phone a few days later, I said to her, "I have some insights about all the things you need to do, and I will share my inner vision, but first I'm going to ask if you'd be willing to do a journey with me?" Her answer was yes. I said, "I want to teach you a new paradigm. I want you to close your eyes." She did as I requested, and I led her into a breathing meditation. Then I said, "I want you to pose a question about the particular energy that's showing up in your life, and I want you to see a symbol for this. After you do this, I want you to come back." When she was done, I said, "Now tell me what your symbol is."

Well, she didn't have just one symbol; she had several. They were a bathtub, a tomato, McDonald's, and a gazebo. She said, "Those symbols don't mean anything to me." At that point I asked her what the bathtub signified to her. I asked her if she took baths, and she said, "No, I take showers." I asked her why she didn't take baths, and she told me that they were too much trouble. I said, "Is that the real reason?" She responded, "Yes, but when I was little I liked the bath because it was such a big tub. Now *I* feel big and it's kind of cumbersome." I asked her what she liked about the tub when she was little. She replied, "It was a place of mystery, and I really liked it. I'd get in there and go under the water, but it was also kind of scary."

"Really? What was scary about it?"

"Well, my dad never paid me very much attention except when I was in the bathtub," she replied. "And it always felt yucky because he paid so much attention to me when I took a bath."

Okay?

And then I said, "Now tell me about the gazebo." She replied, "Well, I went to a gazebo in my neighborhood after we'd moved to town, and it was down behind a house. It was really neat, and I went in, and it was only me. I went in, and I sat down, and I felt really peaceful, and I felt like . . . I just felt the best I'd felt in a long time. But it was also kind of scary because it was behind a house that had been built by prisoners, and apparently a lot of torture took place there."

I sat and thought for a moment, and then I said, "Do you realize that everything you associate with pleasure you also associate with fear and abuse?" And boy was that an eye-opener for her! We discussed it and I said, "Why do you think you can't make decisions on your own? What is the message to you?"

"I was wounded when I was a little kid, and something happened. I think it involved my dad and his inappropriate behavior," she told me. "I don't know if it was actually a case of classic abuse, but there was something unsettling about it. I've lost my confidence, and I'm in a relationship that's not working the way I need it to. My husband . . ." and she continued for a while about her husband. "And I'm depressed and living where it rains all the time, and the gazebo was my safe place, and it's scary to make a decision," and so on and so forth, but the point is that she received all the answers right there herself.

I told her, "With regard to your husband: he is refusing to work on himself, and you thought things would change once you got married, but they haven't. You feel like you're drowning in a place where it rains all the time, and that's a form of physical punishment for you, because you clearly want and crave the sun. You want to be in a safe place, and you want to be in a magical place. You need to do some inner work to heal your codependency with your husband, and you need to make a decision to either confront him and help him get help or get out." And she said, "You got all that?" And I said, "You told me every bit of it."

And that was in an hour's time over the phone, and I had met this girl once for five minutes at a bookstore. I didn't remember her name, but I remembered her face. Before we even began speaking, I tapped in to her energy, and I had pretty much been able to read all of what she eventually put together herself.

"How do I keep this going?" she asked. "How can I continue to do my inner work?" I replied, "You can come to one of my workshops. You can also, on your own, do some breathwork; I know you have my book." (My book *Shamanic Breathwork* includes a CD, which allows the reader to go on a breathwork journey if they so desire.) "You can also discuss the work you are doing with someone, a good friend who you trust. And you can start sitting two or three times a week—just sit and close your eyes and go inside and ask your inner self what it wants to tell you. Ask it what the symbols are that you need to interpret in order to learn what's going on in your life, and how to take the next right step. When you are done meditating, write down those symbols and then sit quietly again and ask yourself what they mean to you. Then write the answers down. And, because it always helps to share, share your process with somebody; this makes all of it more real."

These are the things people can do to begin their inner work.

## DOING THE WORK

When encouraging people to do inner work, a problem often arises: people don't like to hear the word *work*. They don't like to hear *breathwork,* and they don't like to hear *inner work*. This happens because so many people are engaged in professional work that they dislike, and they associate inner work with that. But when you're doing "the great work"—or as Carl Jung called it "the great opus"—it's the work of your soul, and it feels quite different from the work of the ego.

Although initially it may be difficult to discipline yourself to do your inner work, eventually it becomes a joy. As you begin to meditate more regularly or do breathwork sessions and use your shamanic psychospiritual muscles, after a while it becomes a habit and a type of healthy maintenance program of self-care. It's like eating square meals, getting the requisite hours of sleep each night, taking a bath, or brushing your teeth. Everything becomes a part of your routine. Pretty soon it's not even work anymore; it's just a natural part of who you are.

I co-created *The Anubis Oracle* card deck with Nicki Scully and Kris Waldherr to help people learn divination. Working with the laws of synchronicities in the cards can help people make decisions. This is not about fortune telling; it's about learning how to read the road signs along the way and interpret them for your journey. This all becomes part of your lexicon, a language of the soul, but it is inner work. If it makes you feel free and alive, then it can be a joy to do, even if you hit a tough block or have to uncover something that is keeping you stuck.

Indigenous peoples sometime refer to the archetypical imaginal dream world as the land of spirit. This is the place into which spirit downloads from the original One Source. When we do our inner work, we are able to tap into these imaginal realms, and what a rich world it is! And how depleted we are when we aren't in touch with this world, and how soulless we become. If everyone were in touch with this inner world, we wouldn't be doing things like dropping bombs remotely from drone aircraft. Being disconnected from the spirit world is one of the main reasons why soldiers fighting face to face in Iraq and Afghanistan are returning home with such severe PTSD: because they've been forced to do things that violate their spirit, that ravage and dehumanize them, and becoming soulless in the process, they want to die themselves. Soul loss is increasing the rate of veteran suicides daily. It's very important to be in touch with these imaginal realms in order to have access to spirit and to draw our futures to us more quickly.

Another way to learn from the future and to draw our future to us more quickly is through the power of ritual held in sacred space. It's important to know that whenever you put your full intention and attention into a ritual, you are invoking and activating the imaginal cells and calling them into reality. I've known for a long time that when we do rituals and ceremonies we're parting the veils and opening the shamanic portals of possibility. You could say we're calling in the gods, or calling in supernatural help, but we are also actually calling in our future DNA and expanded ka body. We are the future ancestors, and the future manifestation of who we are lives within that memory. When we call in the imaginal cells, sometimes they show up in our life the very next day. That has frequently happened to me, and I have witnessed it hundreds of times in other people's lives.

When you perform the ritual of getting married, for example, you are calling in the future. During the ceremony you call in the future of that marriage. You make commitments: you agree to tell the truth, you agree to trust your partner and to stick with them through thick and thin. You're saying these vows in the present, but you're also talking about the future. That's part of the effect of ritual and ceremony—they solidify something in the moment about what comes next in our lives, and yet we have to move into our future for their real power to resonate and manifest.

When we took initiates through shamanic rituals during our time in Egypt in 2005, we did so with the understanding that the magical transformation that was invoked would continue long after they returned home. We knew that the effects of the renewal of the heart rituals would be long-lasting and that people's lives would continue to transform for a long time to come.

When Brad and I returned from Egypt, it slowly dawned on me that people could go through all of these shamanic initiations without ever having to set foot on Egyptian soil. People everywhere could have these same experiences and be awakened by these archetypal deities by going through similar initiations, which would benefit their lives and call in their renewed hearts. The renewed heart is the future of our Earth.

My heart was symbolically taken out at Sakkara. At Edfu my heart was reactivated by the beat of a drum played by Horus, the spiritual warrior. Even though my heart underwent many renewal rites as we traveled up and down the Nile, I came home with a sense that I was carrying all of this energetically, and working through it again and again with Nicki in a more in-depth and elaborate form over the next couple of years as we coauthored *Shamanic Mysteries of Egypt* and *The Anubis Oracle*. Through the books that we did together, I really felt the rituals unfolding and empowering me and my life, and they continue to unfold in magical and potent ways to this day.

# 13

# Costing Not Less Than Everything

Something really dynamic is happening on Earth right now. We are in the birth canal of a new era, moving from the Piscean age to the Aquarian age, the next level of human consciousness. Whereas the Aquarian age teaches us to own our power, the Piscean Age was an time of devotion—of being dedicated to a guru or a master savior, something outside of oneself. In some sense, from a human evolutionary approach, we can see the appropriateness of that. Children need to be devoted to their parents in order to learn from them. However, one of the problems of authority is the risk of abuse of that sacred trust.

We have all heard horror stories of the spiritual teachers who became corrupt. Witness the child-abuse scandals that have recently rocked the Catholic Church. As the old adage states, absolute power corrupts absolutely. You can see this in prisons where guards abuse the prisoners. They can somehow justify their abusive behavior because the prisoners are known rapists, murderers, and thieves, who according to the guards, deserve to be treated inhumanely.

The same thing happens in slaughterhouses and animal mills. A disturbing story I heard recently had to do with a dairy farm where the workers, who seemed like decent enough people on the face of it, were found to be sticking pitchforks in cows for no reason, and doing other horrible things to the animals on the farm. When the authorities investigated more closely, they found that this didn't happen in just one dairy; the abusive behavior was very widespread.

What makes people be this physically abusive to animals that are providing milk and cheese and butter to the world? There's something very disturbing and wrong when people are cut off from their humanity in this way. We can use the term *humanity* and say that they're cut off from it, but really they're cut off from not only their humanity but also their spiritual essence and their access to the divine source. What has filled in the void is a very sick ego and an extreme narcissism based on low self-worth, which puts the sole focus on the individual and its primal need for survival at the expense of the welfare of the collective whole.

In our society, a sense of powerlessness and hopelessness on the individual level has become epidemic, whether it's manifested by our leaders, our ministers, our service workers, or ourselves. The amount of addiction is also at epidemic levels, whether it's substance abuse, codependency, or a myriad of other addictive patterns. The only way these levels of inhumanity can exist is because people have become very wounded and disembodied.

The way to become embodied is to heal our emotional wounds and reclaim our lost soul parts. There is so much soul loss in individuals today, whether experienced by a child in Iraq who has witnessed the death of his parents, by a woman in Haiti who has lost her home and source of livelihood, or encountered in a more prosaic way each and every day in, as Shakespeare said in *Hamlet,* "the heart-ache and the thousand natural shocks that flesh is heir to . . ."

Peter A. Levine, in his book *Waking the Tiger: Healing Trauma,* says: "Trauma is perhaps the most avoided, ignored, belittled, denied, misunderstood and untreated cause of human suffering." In *Trauma Through a Child's Eyes: Awakening the Ordinary Miracle of Healing,* Levine and coauthor Maggie Kline say, "Trauma is the antithesis of empowerment."

Whatever creates soul loss has generated so *much* soul loss that we've become machines: just eating, breathing, breeding machines. But that's not really who we are; we've lost sight of our true selves, deep down.

Shakespeare said, "This thing of darkness is mine." If we don't own and heal our shadow, then this thing of darkness that is ours individually will not allow us to bring our respective light into the world. I once heard my teacher Jacquie Small say that those who refuse to do their inner work are a plague upon society.

Saint Teresa of Avila wrote a book called *The Interior Castle* in the fourteenth century. In it were these concerns: How is it that we do not know our interior world? Who *are* we really? We answer, well, my mother is so and so, and my father is la de dah, and this is where I live, and this is what I do. Now, that's all an important part of our human story but only a small, exterior part. Who are we really? *Inside?*

We all need to be courageous enough to acknowledge that part of ourselves that lives in darkness. We all need to face our sadness, our anger, and our disappointment in order to bring healing to the parts of ourselves that we consistently repress and deny.

It's important to know that the imaginal self cannot be destroyed, even when the human self dies. The imaginal self still exists, and I believe that is why people reincarnate. Each incarnation gives us another opportunity to try to download who we really are. As the ego transforms, our soul purpose is born—and there's a deep enrichment that comes from being soul-filled, or being soulful. Soulful people have done and continue to do their inner work; they are very conscious and very connected to spirit.

## CHANGE AS A PREREQUISITE FOR SURVIVAL

As a global community, humankind is approaching a time of unprecedented challenges, unique in our recorded history. To meet these challenges successfully, we will have to shift our thinking from an ego-based paradigm to a heart- and spirit-based one if we are to survive.

In his book *The Meaning of the 21ˢᵗ Century,* James Martin says,

> At the start of the 21st century, humankind finds itself on a non-sustainable course—a course that, unless it is changed, could lead to grand-scale catastrophes. . . . We live on a small, beautiful and totally isolated planet, but its population is becoming too large; enormous new consumer societies are growing, of which China is the largest; and technology is becoming powerful enough to wreck the planet. We are traveling at breakneck speed into an age of extremes—extremes in wealth and poverty, extremes in technology and the experiments that scientists want to perform, extreme forces of globalism, weapons of mass destruction and terrorists acting in the name of religion. If we are to survive, we have to learn how to manage this situation. . . . This could be either humanity's last century or the century that sets the world on a course toward a spectacular future.

He goes on to say, "We can look at the future in one of two ways. We can ask: What is *the right thing to do?* Or we can ask: What is *the most likely thing to happen?*"

What is the right thing to do?

Where do we look to determine what is the right thing to do?

We look into our future selves, and we respond with our *heart's inner knowing and vision.*

By doing our inner work, we get in touch with our hearts. And by getting in touch with our hearts, we do *the right thing.* If we do the right thing, hope is born inside of us because we realize that we have the opportunity to actually save ourselves and our planet from destruction.

As Dr. Stanislav Grof remarked in his acceptance speech for the 2007 Vision 97 award, "One of the most remarkable consequences of various forms of transpersonal experiences is spontaneous emergence and development of genuine humanitarian and ecological interests and need to take part in activities aimed at peaceful coexistence and well-being of humanity. . . . As a result of these experiences, individuals tend to develop feelings that they are planetary citizens and members of the human family before belonging to a particular country or a specific racial, social, ideological, political, or religious group."

Our tasks are to remember that we are all deeply connected and to relate collectively for the good of the whole and for future generations. The Native Americans have a saying that reflects their philosophy of preservation: "We are borrowing the Earth from our grandchildren." Our Western culture often reflects the antithesis of this mindset; it's all about "me." As we leave the "Me Generation" behind, we need to truly become the "We Generation."

As I see it, the mandate must become "One for all and all for one," as Grandmother Twylah was fond of saying. This is unity and diversity in a nutshell. We are moving away from the Piscean fourth world, an age of isolation and separation, into the Aquarian fifth world, an age of unity and diversity. In this much heralded new age, if we are all conscious enough, we may discover that the Field of Plenty is actually right here on a new Earth.

## THE NEVERENDING SPIRAL OF TRANSFORMATION

I have found myself struggling with the appropriate ending of this book, mainly because I recently have been in a process wherein many things are dying within me and many things are struggling to be born. I was sick with the flu right after Christmas. This threw me into a two-week health and emotional crisis, which was preceded by old emotional patterns that reared their ugly demonic heads quite abruptly.

It was a particularly emotional visit to my folks' house over the Christmas holidays, and I say this with surprise because the last few years it's as if the lights came on between my parents and me— especially my mother. We have broken the silence on more than one occasion about things that had been left unspoken for years. We made amends and cleared the air. In this, I felt as if I have been seen, heard, and even understood in ways that I had given up on long, long ago.

So when things were harder than usual to deal with during the holidays this year, and there was a highly charged incident between my mother and me regarding the care of my father, it caught me completely off-guard. I suddenly felt sixteen years old again and caught in the middle of my parents' drama. Words were said on both sides, and for a few hours I was not the mature, grown-up daughter that I always try to be with them.

Whenever I think I have it all together and I am in control of everything from here on out, I get another dose of humility, and if I'm not listening, this can become quite humiliating. One of the prescriptions for sober living and continued spiritual growth in the recovery movement is to stay grounded one day at a time, even while we are growing by leaps and bounds spiritually. One of the ways to do that is to keep conscious contact with a higher or greater power, one bigger than the ego, and to keep the ego in proper alignment with our spirit, with a sense of humility.

This means that on an ego level, we have to face the fact that we don't have all the answers. In this, the ego must be willing to undergo an ego death again and again, especially when those imaginal cells call and say, "Hey, sister, it's time for a change."

So, much to my dismay, I found myself in a regressed state shortly before I left my folks' house, and simultaneously Brad got sick with a nasty fever and cold on our drive back to North Carolina. Of course, I cared for him during that two-day trip. By the time we arrived home, he was feeling better, but by then I was starting to go down, and down I went—and hard. I took on the bug, and it got me much more severely and for a longer period of time than it ever thought about getting Brad.

I can't help but think that the incident with my family helped to create the perfect environment in my body and psyche for the illness to take root, and the opportunity to release something at a deeper cellular level was activated.

My friends around the country sent me a lot of support including some pretty entertaining e-mails. A friend who goes by the name Sheewho, who knows me and my work fairly well, is aware that I am fascinated by the symbol of the butterfly and the imaginal cells. She started sending me funny statements such as "Who will win—the flu bug or the butterfly?" and "It's the fight of the century, the battle between the bug and the butterfly!" As I sat with these jokes, it dawned on me that although this was intended to be funny, the shadow is often best seen in what is humorous or ridiculous in our lives.

The lesson of the shadow becomes rather obvious when we can lighten up, laugh at ourselves, and not take things so seriously. So during this time, I imagined that my immune system was not only fighting off the flu bug but also trying to destroy the imaginal cells. It was doing this because it didn't understand that they bubbled up on purpose during my relapse into a family of origin episode in order to help me rebirth yet another level of consciousness on my evolutionary spiral path and deepen my connection with the Tree of Life.

I spent several days, because I was down for the count anyway, just lying in bed, doing what breathwork I was able to summon up within my congested lungs, and listening to Shamanic Breathwork journey music. Each time, the growing image of the Tree of Life swirled around my mind's eye, and I felt myself dropping deeply into the still waters of life to meet a symbolic death and make peace with it. As I embraced my shamanic death by symbolically becoming Osiris, I knew it was time to simply be still and listen as I slowly dissolved and turned into caterpillar mush.

In so doing I felt myself developing a deeper empathy for the little caterpillar and his demise, as his higher form sought to emerge from the goo. I imagined my immune system becoming overwhelmed with the new energies downloading into my energy field, and I could feel the resistance of the old self as it reluctantly started to release its grip on a way of being that was familiar, even if outworn. When you are in this state, it doesn't matter that you may not know exactly what you are letting go of. You just need to accept that whatever you are giving up is no longer a part of who you are becoming.

I have gotten very comfortable with who I have become over the past few years. My personal life and spiritual work in the world have brought me great satisfaction, and yet lately I have felt that something else has been stirring just beneath the surface, preparing to rise into my awareness. Rob, a spiritual brother of mine, once said, "It's one thing to let go of negative things in one's life; it's quite another to let go of things that actually seem to be working in order to grow toward another level of consciousness simply because it's the right thing to do and it's time!"

## THE FIRE AND THE ROSE

So, here I sit, as is so often the case, deeply within the very process I am immersed in writing about. I am not a stranger to this journey; in fact, I eat, sleep, live, and teach this journey; I guide others through it; it influences everything I do. This spiral path is the very foundation of the teachings at Venus Rising and our university, and it is the basis for all our shamanic programs. I too am faced with the eternal questions: Who am I becoming now? What am I letting go of this time? Where am I headed on the spiral path of transformation?

A few lines from one of my favorite poems, "Little Gidding," from *Four Quartets*, by T. S. Eliot, are as follows:

> *Quick now, here, now, always—*
> *A condition of complete simplicity*
> *(Costing not less than everything)*
> *And all shall be well and*
> *All manner of thing shall be well.*
> *When the tongues of flame are in-folded*
> *Into the crowned knot of fire*
> *And the fire and the rose are one.*

## A PARTY FOR THE EARTH

Last night I spent time in my dreams with Grandmother Twylah, as I have many times before. It seems that since her passing to the other side of the veil, I have felt an even stronger connection than I did the last few years of her earthly life. In one dream, all the spiritual teachers I have ever known, as well as many I have never met, came together to participate in a huge healing ceremony for the earth and its peoples.

Tremendous excitement filled the air, and I felt a bit out of place, but this didn't faze Grandma Twylah, who was her usual good-natured but no-nonsense, straightforward self. Drums and flutes were carried into a healing circle, and beautiful feathers of all kinds were strung about, along with prayer flags from many different nations and religions. I caught sight of the Dalai Lama and Grandmother Twylah out of the corner of my eye, off by themselves, laughing secretly like children as they mischievously planned some grand surprise for the special gathering.

At one point Gram told me to make sure that all the folks coming had a comfortable place to lie down so they could do an inner shamanic journey with breathwork and to check the music system and call the musicians together. She loved music and loved to see folks connect with the sacred breath and change their lives for the better, as well as help change the world by becoming "real human beings."

She also told me that much healing would be performed on the planet, by many different healers and teachers of every imaginal kind during this gathering of all nations. All those who loved the earth had heard the call, from the farthest reaches of the universe and every dimension of consciousness, and they were coming to assist every being on Earth.

What a grand gathering this was to be! I was not sure what my role was except to keep paying attention by listening, to follow the instructions provided by one wiser than me, and to do my part to help it all come together. In the dream, I wanted to see more, I wanted to know the outcome, but it was clear I was simply supposed to show up, do my part, trust the outcome, and let go. Although my ego wanted more information, my heart trusted the process, and I knew that in good time all would be revealed and all would be well.

So that is where I leave you, dear reader, and myself as well . . . within the chrysalis and much like Osiris in his sarcophagus, coming apart while trusting that something within, perhaps the Great Mother Isis herself, remembers our original blueprint. She will see us through as our hearts are truly renewed, as we travel this amazing journey of activating our imaginal cells, re-creating our ka bodies, and trusting that there is a sacred plan for all of humanity and this enchanted Earth. We are not here by accident. We have a Divine Appointment. We are right here, right now, on purpose, in the middle of Earth's transformation, and the timing is perfect.

# About Venus Rising Programs

Linda Star Wolf is the founder of the **Venus Rising Association for Transformation**, a 501c3 nonprofit spiritual organization dedicated to transforming personal and planetary consciousness and supporting people in truly stepping into their soul purpose. Venus Rising offers many exciting spiritual teachings, gatherings, celebrations, and ceremonies at their five elemental temples, as well as degree programs, certifications, personal transformation retreats, trainings, and workshops at the **Isis Cove Community and Retreat Center**, in the beautiful blue mountains of western North Carolina, and at events around the country and abroad.

**Venus Rising University for Shamanic Psychospiritual Studies** is one of the first shamanic psychospiritual universities in the world, offering shamanic wisdom teachings and principles that support the integration of the ego, soul, and spirit. The curriculum is structured to accelerate personal growth and leadership and to provide a challenging and exciting perspective on how to embody a spiritual career that has heart and gives meaning and purpose to your life.

One of the main tools for transformation used at Venus Rising is **Shamanic Breathwork**. This process was created by Star Wolf to help people connect to their own inner visionary shaman, clear out the blocks to wholeness, and make the real and sustainable changes they wish to embody in their lives.

**The Shamanic Ministers' Global Network** is a worldwide association of shamanic ministers ordained through the Venus Rising Association for Transformation. While individual shamanic ministers within this global network use many different tools to awaken shamanic awareness within those around them, all begin with the core belief that a visionary shaman lives within each and every one of us and that holding a deeply personal and creative relationship with that direct connection to the One Source will help create a better world.

**The Shamanic Healing Initiatory Process (SHIP)** is a series of five shamanic initiations at the core of everything taught at Venus Rising. The five initiations are: The Five Cycles of Shamanic Consciousness and the Spiral Path of Alchemical Transformation, The Family of Origin, Dancing with the Shadow, Embracing the Divine Beloved, and Discovering Sacred Soul Purpose. These initiations are designed to help people open up to a powerful portal of transformation, release the blocks to wholeness, access their own inner visionary shaman, and step into a life of passion and purpose.

**The Transformation House Shamanic Soul Recovery Process** is a program for those desiring to deepen their spiritual connection, open to their sacred purpose, move through rites of passage such as the transition from one phase of life to another, work on self-defeating behavior patterns, or deepen their recovery beyond addictions and relapse prevention. Transformation House was designed for anyone wishing to experience a deeper level of intensive mind-body-spirit rejuvenation away from the routines of daily life.

If you are ready to transform your life, contact us to discuss the right Venus Rising program to meet your needs:

**www.shamanicbreathwork.org**
**venusrising@shamanicbreathwork.org**
**(828) 631-2305**

# BIBLIOGRAPHY

*Alice in Wonderland.* DVD. Directed by Tim Burton. The Walt Disney Company, 2010.

Arrien, Angeles. "Four Ways to Wisdom." SpiritSound. www.spiritsound.com/arrien.html (accessed July 7, 2011).

*Avatar.* DVD. Directed by James Cameron. Twentieth Century Fox, 2009.

Bauval, Robert, and Adrian Gilbert. *The Orion Mystery: Unlocking the Secrets of the Pyramids.* New York: Three Rivers Press, 1995.

Benedict, Mellen-Thomas. "Near-Death Experience NDE Story of Mellen-Thomas Benedict: Journey Through the Light and Back." Mellen-Thomas Benedict. www.mellen-thomas.com/stories.htm (accessed February 10, 2011).

Brook, Timothy. *Vermeer's Hat: The Seventeenth Century and the Dawn of the Global World.* New York: Bloomsbury, 2007.

Clow, Barbara Hand. *The Mayan Code: Time Acceleration and Awakening the World Mind.* Rochester, Vt.: Bear & Company, 2007.

———. *The Mind Chronicles: A Visionary Guide into Past Lives.* Rochester, Vt.: Bear & Company, 2007.

Eliot, T. S. *T. S. Eliot: Collected Poems, 1909–1962.* New York: Harcourt Brace Jovanovich, 1991.

Ellis, Normandi. *Awakening Osiris: The Egyptian Book of the Dead.* San Francisco: Red Wheel/Weiser, 2009.

———. *Dreams of Isis: A Woman's Spiritual Sojourn.* Wheaton, Ill.: Quest Books, 1995.

———. *Feasts of Light: Celebrations for the Seasons of Life based on the Egyptian Goddess Mysteries.* Wheaton, Ill.: Quest Books, 1999.

Falconer, Ruby, and Linda Star Wolf. *Shamanic Eygptian Astrology: Your Planetary Relationship to the Gods.* Rochester, Vt.: Bear & Company, 2010.

*Food, Inc.* DVD. Directed by Robert Kenner. Magnolia Home Entertainment, 2008.

Fox, Matthew. *Original Blessing: A Primer in Creation Spirituality Presented in Four Paths, Twenty-Six Themes, and Two Questions.* New York: Tarcher, 2000.

Harvey, Andrew. *The Hope: A Guide to Sacred Activism.* Carlsbad, Calif.: Hay House, 2009.

Levine, Peter A. *Waking the Tiger: Healing Trauma.* Berkeley, Calif.: North Atlantic Books, 1997.

Levine, Peter A., and Maggie Kline. *Trauma Through a Child's Eyes: Awakening the Ordinary Miracle of Healing.* Berkeley, Calif.: North Atlantic Books, 2006.

Martin, James. *The Meaning of the 21st Century: An Urgent Plan for Ensuring Our Future.* New York: Riverhead Trade, 2007.

———. *Technology's Crucible.* Upper Saddle River, N.J.: Prentice Hall, 1987.

———. *The Wired Society: A Challenge for Tomorrow.* Upper Saddle River, N.J.: Prentice Hall, 1978.

Newton, Michael. *Destiny of Souls: New Case Studies of Life Between Lives.* Woodbury, Minn.: Llewellyn, 2000.

———. *Journey of Souls: Case Studies of Life Between Lives.* Woodbury, Minn.: Llewellyn, 1994.

Ruiz, Don Miguel. *The Four Agreements: A Practical Guide to Personal Freedom.* San Rafael, Calif.: Amber-Allen Publishing, 1997.

Scully, Nicki. *Alchemical Healing: A Guide to Spiritual, Physical, and Transformational Medicine.* Rochester, Vt.: Bear & Company, 2003.

Scully, Nicki, and Mark Hallert. *Planetary Healing: Spirit Medicine for Global Transformation.* Rochester, Vt.: Bear & Co., 2011.

Scully, Nicki, and Linda Star Wolf. *The Anubis Oracle: A Journey into the Shamanic Mysteries of Egypt.* Rochester, Vt.: Bear & Company, 2008.

———. *Shamanic Mysteries of Egypt: Awakening the Healing Power of the Heart.* Rochester, Vt.: Bear & Company, 2007.

Star Wolf, Linda. *Shamanic Breathwork: Journeying Beyond the Limits of the Self.* Rochester, Vt.: Bear & Company, 2009.

Teresa of Avila (Saint). *The Interior Castle.* Charleston, S.C.: CreateSpace, 2010.

Tolle, Eckhart. *A New Earth: Awakening to Your Life's Purpose.* New York: Penguin Books, 2008.

# İNDEX

Page numbers in *italics* refer to illustrations.

# How to Use the CD

The *Visionary Shamanism Musical Journeys* CD features Matt Venuti's distinctive compositions and improvisations. The featured instruments include the custom-designed Electronic Valve Instrument (EVI) and the Hang, a contemporary instrument with timeless qualities. *Hang* means "hand" in the Swiss-German Bernese dialect, and the Hang in Matt's hands is pure magic.

The music will support you in engaging at a higher level of consciousness as you journey to your future selves. Shamanic Breathwork and Matt's music come together with a magical alchemy that awakens and activates the Visionary Shaman within and promotes a journey for downloading your imaginal cells from the greater field of being.

You may choose to use one of the first three tracks on the CD to journey for about 15 minutes, or you can listen to the entire CD at once and journey for about an hour. Listening to the CD as you go to sleep at night will also help activate and download your imaginal cells. Please do not use the CD while driving a car or operating heavy machinery.

Here are some recommendations for embarking on your Visionary Shamanism musical journey!

- Set aside fifteen minutes to an hour for your journey, plus some time at the end to make some artwork, write in your journal, and ground yourself. We also recommend that you share your journey and visions with someone else, perhaps a soul friend or even a group of others who take the musical journey with you.

- Set up a private, quiet, comfortable space. Make sure the phones are off and that you won't be distracted. Clear the space of furniture so that if you want to move around during your journey you can safely do so. Make a comfortable mat to lie down on with blankets and pillows.

- Have the CD at hand and ready to play along with a journal and perhaps some art supplies and paper so that after your journey you can record your experience in words, images, symbols, and colors.

- If you would like to create your journey as a ritual, you might light a candle, lower the lights, and burn some sage or incense. Offer up your prayers or intentions to spirit, to your higher power or to your highest self. Call upon any spirit guides or other helpers to escort and assist you during your Visionary Shamanism journey.

- Make yourself comfortable on your mat, begin to slow your breathing and take a few minutes to relax your entire body. Turn on the CD, then just lie back on your mat and begin to breathe in and out to the music at your own pace. Breathe until you are surprised, allowing your feelings and sensations to emerge and release. Allow your body to move around in any way that you are guided and embrace your life-force energy, visions, and activations.

- The first track will start you on your journey and activate your first three chakras. The second track will take you into the heart of the matter by activating your fourth chakra. The third track will activate your upper chakras. The fourth track is an upbeat song that Matt created called "We're All In This Together"; it celebrates your transformative experience and will assist you in coming fully back from the journey. The vitality of the fourth track may inspire you to get up and dance. If you prefer to lie still and rest, you may wish to turn the CD off after the third track. When you feel ready, slowly begin to return to your outer reality and your normal breathing and awareness.

- After your journey, you may want to write in your journal or make some art to illustrate your experience. Drink plenty of water and eat a snack to ground yourself. Try not to rush back into regular life until you have fully grounded yourself; it is easy to underestimate the altered state in which you may still find yourself. Take some time to call a friend or confidant. Speaking about your experience out loud and having it witnessed is an important part of integrating your experience.

• In the days following your journey, keep your artwork out where you can see it and your journal close at hand so that you can continue to make notes about your new consciousness and visions. Pay close attention to how your experience may be showing up in synchronistic ways around you in the world.

May this be a magical, musical journey for you as your Visionary Shaman awakens and your imaginal cells are activated. Be sure to celebrate the birth of your imaginal cells and then take action to embody your visions in a sacred way.

We're all in this together!

STAR WOLF AND MATT VENUTI

### *"We're All In This Together" Lyrics (CD Track 4)*
Words and Music by Matt Venuti

*Taoist Buddist Muslim Jew Christian Hindu chosen few*
*Temple burnin' atheism, Burnin' Man paganism,*
*Bugs bats birds cats trees fleas dogs rats,*
*Child bearin' those without, single/married, gangs, scouts*

*We're all in this together*
*We're all in this together*
*We're all in this together*
*The Rhythm Of Life*

*Squeelers dealers touchy feelers snow mobilers 4 wheelers,*
*Limos bikes queens serfs unemployed and those who work,*
*Freedom fighters yoga teachers armadillos forest creatures*
*Walkers skippers swimmers runners saints strippers singers*
  *drummers*

*We're all in this together*
*We're all in this together*
*We're all in this together*
*The Rhythm Of Life*

*Village people city dwellers country folk gals & fellers*
*Gay bi straight tolerate love hate*
*Homeless genius black yellow white brown red*
*Stars Mars Venus gas pure tainted living dead*

*Public supported local imported completion aborted*
*Clean and distorted*
*Friends and enemies women and men*
*Heaven and hell beginning and end*
*The rich the poor the meek and the proud*
*The land the sea the air and the clouds*
*The future the past the here and the now*
*Say it inside say it out loud*

*We're all in this together*
*We're all in this together*
*We're all in this together*
*The Rhythm Of Life*

As a composer and performer, multi-instrumentalist Matt Venuti has made unique contributions to contemporary music genres. He and his band, The Venusians, are known for combining traditional and contemporary instrumentation and performing worldwide.

As a soloist, Matt tours with the Hang, unfolding a soulful musical journey of rhythm, melody, and resonance.

Please visit **www.mattvenuti.com** for more information.